# Film The

## For Beginners

PUBLISHED BY

Zidane Press,
25 Shaftesbury Road,
London N19 4QW

First edition 2014
Printed by Page Bros, Norwich, UK.

Text Copyright © 2014 Richard Osborne
Illustrations Copyright © 2014 Angie Brew
Cover Copyright © 2014 Angie Brew and Peter Hudson
Book Design by Peter Hudson

Richard Osborne and Angie Brew are to be identified as
the authors of this work, and have asserted their rights in
accordance with the Copyright, Designs and Patent Act 1988.

A CIP catalogue record of this book is available
from the British Library.

ISBN-10: 0956267866

DISTRIBUTED BY

Turnaround Publisher Services Ltd,
Unit 3 Olympia Trading Estate,
Coburg Road, Wood Green,
London N22 6TZ
Phone: +44(0) 20 8829 3019

# Film Theory
## For Beginners

**Richard Osborne & Angie Brew**

 ZIDANE PRESS

# How to use this book

Film theory is an enormous, very complicated topic. *Film Theory for Beginners* is intended as a very general introduction to some of the basic ideas and theorists. It is therefore rather broad in its explanations. It is intended 'for beginners', to demonstrate some of the arguments. We have used many quotations from film theorists and filmmakers so where a quotation says Bazin (for example) then that is a direct quote from the person themself. We have used a film script format for these quotes from theorists and filmmakers, and also as a device for dialogue between an imaginary student and professor. Students, you need to read the people themselves and to think about the pleasure of film in all its complexities. *Film Theory for Beginners* should point you in the direction of the main debates.

Draw to Learn: The drawings are a spontaneous response to the text. We hope that they will encourage readers to make their own additional drawings, to explore the power of drawing as a learning tool. For more information on why and how to draw please visit brewdrawing.com.

# Contents

# Chapter 1 Background and main approaches

A FRAME

A SHOT

A SCENE

So why would anybody want to study film?

Or complicate matters by having a theory of film?

What is a film and how do we define it?

STUDENT

Some people argue that, since films are mere entertainment, you just watch them and enjoy them. So why do we have a theory of film?

PROFESSOR

Most importantly because film is probably the biggest cultural change in 2,000 years and is undeniably the most important cultural form of the twentieth and twenty-first centuries.

STUDENT
But why is it such a big
**cultural change?**

PROFESSOR
Because watching moving images, which
**led to film and TV and transformed**
everybody's sense of the world,
made the whole world accessible to
everyone and led to a totally new
form of popular culture - that is,
**watching films.** Now movies are a
huge part of global entertainment,
**and everybody watches films,** maybe
2 billion people a week.

STUDENT
Ok, I get the importance.
**But why film theory?**

PROFESSOR
Because thinking **about how films are**
made, watched and understood means
analyzing how culture works overall,
which is essential to understanding
how people and society work. If you
are interested in culture you have to
**be interested in film.** You can analyze
how films are made, edited and
distributed, as well as the people who
watch them. Also of interest are the
people who **criticize films and audience**
reactions.

The people who
make them

The people
who edit them

The people who
watch them

and also the people who
criticize them

STUDENT
So can we have a summary of
what film theory is about?

PROFESSOR
Well I suppose it is an academic
theory about how we watch and
understand films, and how they
work, and produce meanings.

STUDENT
But that is a bit general.

PROFESSOR
OK, well to try and summarize it
formally we can say — film theory is
an important new academic discipline
that was developed in the later
part of the twentieth century and
which aims to explore the essence of
what cinema is, and what it tries
to do. Most importantly it seeks to
provide a conceptual framework for
understanding film's relationship to
social reality, to the other visual
arts, and to literature, as well as
to individual viewers, and to society
in general. In other words it is an
overall attempt to theorize what
making and viewing films is all about.

STUDENT
So understanding film means utilizing
a theory of film which can explain
what film is, where it came from
and what it can do, and linking the
different aspects of film together.

What is real?

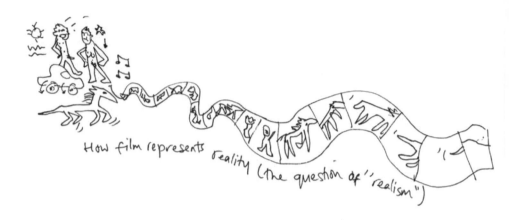

How film represents reality (the question of "realism")

Key questions are: How film represents reality...

# Chapter 2 Early development and key questions

## Some key questions in film theory are:

- On what basis do we discuss the significance of film?
- Which is more important, the form of a film or its function?
- Does film represent reality?
- Is film an entirely separate and new art form?
- What is its relationship to 'high art' and 'low art'?
- Is film naturally realistic?
- Is 'naturalism' what film does best?
- Is film a language that has a grammar, form and structure?
- How does film deal with fantasy, the unconscious and dreams?
- How do audiences understand films and their meaning?
- Is there a way of describing what a 'perfect' film would be?
- What is the contemporary role of film?
- Are film and television, and other forms of screen entertainment, coalescing?

Overall, film theory has to try and deal with the complexity of how film is made, edited, screened, experienced, consumed and understood, so it has to be a new kind of theory that brings all of these elements together. That is probably why film theory took so long to develop. It started mostly talking about the aesthetics bit but later developed into a broader theory. So first we can look at the broad categories that underpin film theory (and philosophy) and then we can look at the history of how film theory developed and changed over the last 120 years (don't forget how new film is in terms of human artistic development). This chapter outlines the basic things to look at in film theory.

## Institutions

Film is completely different from all previous visual art forms because it is basically social and collaborative - its production and consumption are irredeemably social. Filmmaking is a co-operative, complex and expensive process, so in most circumstances it can only be done by institutions, not individuals. The way these institutions are organized profoundly affects the sorts of films that are made, for example when governments run film industries then it is usually propaganda that gets made. The Hollywood 'studio system' was one such set of institutions.

Institutions are the organizations and people who work in them and the operational processes and practices that define moving-image media production and use. Hollywood makes films that make money and does so by making 'entertainment', which is a particular type of film. Without these institutions, there would be no film or media. There are many different kinds of institutions from Hollywood to Bollywood, and many kinds of global media industries, from Fox, Disney, News Corporation through to Google and Amazon, as well as the various national film and television industries, the computer games industry, the newspaper industry, and the new multi-media conglomerates. The nature of film production and consumption is changing along with the changing nature of institutions. There is some independent filmmaking but it is relatively small-scale.

PRODUCTION –

24 shots per second..

POLITICS          ECONOMICS          CULTURAL IDEAS

Does ownership and control of media institutions give power to control the output, the ideas and forms of film?

7

are the means and mechanisms by which film is created and projected.

## Technologies

From the first moving image camera to the internet, the possibilities of what technology can do has always affected how films can be made and shown – to some it is the most important aspect. Technological determinism is the name given to the theory that technology is all-important.

Technologies are simply the means and mechanisms by which film is created and screened. These technologies are used to create meaning in moving-image film production and consumption. From cameras to lighting, film stock and editing machines, through to projectors, and later the sound recording technologies, the machinery of actual film production has defined what was possible, or achievable in movies. Originally making films was a very difficult business and projecting them also, but as technology improved (and it did very quickly) things got easier and cinema spread like wildfire across the globe. For example, sound technology destroyed the silent film and we can probably say that hand-held cameras messed up the studio system.

Media technologies are the tools that allow media products to be produced, distributed and accessed. Today technology is driving movie production, and media convergence, at an extraordinary pace.

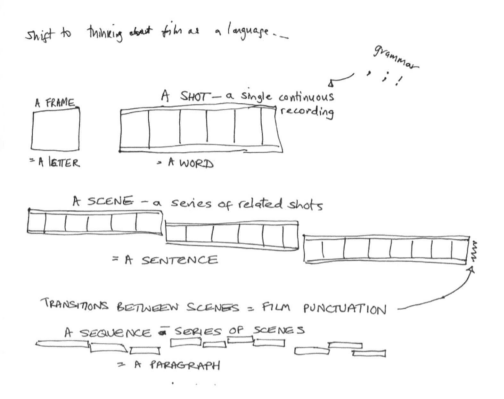

Shift to thinking about film as a language ._

grammar

, ; !

A FRAME

A SHOT — a single continuous recording

= A LETTER

= A WORD

A SCENE — a series of related shots

= A SENTENCE

TRANSITIONS BETWEEN SCENES = FILM PUNCTUATION

A SEQUENCE = SERIES OF SCENES

= A PARAGRAPH

JOHN LASSETER
The art challenges the technology,
and the technology inspires the art.

# Languages

There is a question as to whether film is a 'universal language' that transcends all other cultural forms (this was particularly argued of silent film). This idea started very early on in film theory. Thinking about film as a language (which has its own grammar) is an important historical shift in film studies. It means thinking about the way films convey meaning. Thinking about film as a kind of language was a big move in film theory, and we'll come back to it later.

Languages are systems of **signs and symbols** that are organized through codes and conventions to create meaning.

We can say that **media languages** are the elements that form the building blocks of contemporary communication. These include the rules, sometimes called codes, relating to the technical, symbolic and narrative aspects of media.

The **technical codes** include modes of presentation, the shot types, camera angles, lighting, framing and composition, the editing style, and the use of different elements of sound.

**Symbolic codes** (means of communication) are the elements such as body language, props and costumes, lighting effects, facial expression, location design, codes of dialogue and the patterns of showing situations in the films.

**Narrative codes** are the organized patterns (structures) of the way that the story is constructed: 'Once upon a time' etc. All films are constructed in particular ways that convey specified types of meaning - through the narrative codes. Film theory looks to deconstruct how these forms of communication work at the level of the plot.

## So, we need to analyze film as narrative and how things signify.

COWBOY
Those damn injuns are sending
up smoke signals again.

# Audiences

The film audience was originally a very large, and mostly lower-class audience, as film was seen as rather vulgar. The mass audience was mostly thought of as being pretty much just that, a mass. Somewhere along the way somebody began to realize that there could be different audiences for different films, so the theory of audiences and reception was born, although this was slow to develop.

## So, what is an audience?

It is the individuals and groups of people for whom films are made, and who make meanings when they use these products. Hollywood has a pretty good idea of the audience it is aiming its products at, although interestingly with film, they often get it wrong. The history of film flops is a fascinating one. (The making of **Cleopatra** is probably the funniest of all). 'Know your audience' is a kind of media mantra, but it doesn't always work.

For film theory, it becomes a question of how you define audiences, how you understand them and of thinking about the way that people use film products in many ways, sometimes not intended by the producers. While films are often perfectly directed towards their target audience, like teenage movies, many fail because they are simply rejected by the audience. In the contemporary world media audiences now are also becoming producers themselves, creating and distributing content via websites, blogs, YouTube, and other digital forums. So for film theory the question of an audience just got a whole lot more complicated.

Within this basic theoretical framework, we can now try and look at the history of the development of film theory, whilst recognizing that most film theory is a partial description of a complicated process.

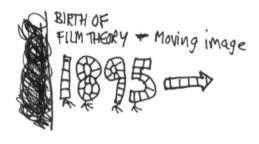

## The birth of film theory

With many subjects, like philosophy or art, for instance, it is quite hard to say when they began. (Art could be 500,000 years old, for example.) Film theory is quite different. We have a very specific starting date: 1895.

Film, or moving image, began in December 1895 when the Lumière brothers publicly showed the very first moving image film. (There are many precursors and lots of technological debate but basically most people agree that this was the first proper 'film'.) Photography was a pre-cursor but film as we know it began then.

'Louis Lumière'

c. 50s    50s    50s

10 short films of about 50s each

←·LE CINEMATOGRAPHE

# What is film theory?

At its simplest it is an explanation of how films get made, and at its most complex it is a set of ideas about how you analyze the production and consumption of films, or how they produce meaning and effect. Then there is the question of whether the technology of film is critical, or the ideas that are in a film.

So what IS Film Theory?

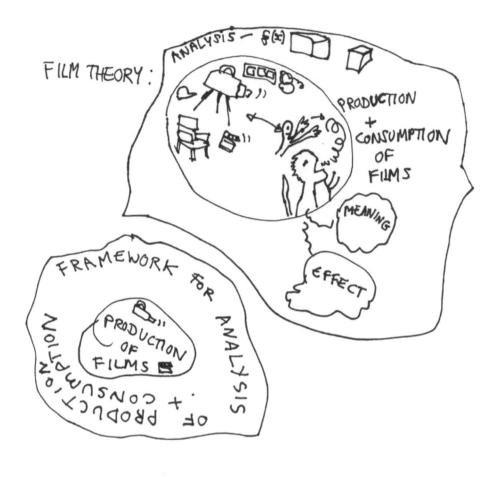

Can we argue that film is a uniquely modern
thing, which almost comes out of nowhere?

Most other cultural forms, like, for example, the novel, have their roots in much, much older practices (like long poems) but film suddenly pops up like nobody's business out of the void. Film is therefore a truly modern invention.

Now it seems almost as though it is the most natural thing in the world, but back then it was incredibly new and somewhat odd. The Lumière brothers didn't think it had much of a future. They thought it was just a minor fad!

These two pioneering brothers worked for their Dad who sold standard photographic equipment and through that background knowledge they got into thinking about the technologies that were around at the time and they came up with what they called the Le Cinematographe (1895) which recorded and showed moving images.

At first Louis Lumière simply filmed the world around him through his camera and took everyday subjects, like his workers. The first private screening of their motion pictures was held on December 28th, 1895 at the Salon Indien du Grand Café in Paris (the downstairs bit). This fairly momentous event - and we don't know who was there - was a presentation of 10 short films of about 50 seconds each.

Their world directorial debut was *La Sortie des Usines Lumière (Workers Leaving the Lumière Factory)*. These pictures of people going home look quite mundane but basically these short films were the arrival of a new dawn in the arts: the cinema.

These very early films simply showed people doing everyday things, and that, because it was such a revolutionary technical process, was fascinating. Only later did people start to think about the sort of stories that film could tell, or of what film could be used for, and thus began film narrative, and film theory.

The shock of seeing oneself in moving time probably kept people occupied for at least the first five years. Then people rapidly began to adjust to the 'movies' – and that part of film theory is thinking about how people began to explore this new medium and its possibilities.

Once films started to tell stories, and filmmakers started to charge money to watch the films, then film as an institution got started – and thus the complexities of film theory also began to develop.

Film as an institution –

Technologies

Communication of meaning –

Textual analysis

This is the beginning of film theory debates

What is fascinating is the realization that film could begin to represent the world in many complex ways that went much further than still images and the written word. It was a truly revolutionary art.

If you think about the early beginnings of film you can see the ways in which it had to draw on past ideas and ways of doing things. Film had been born but it wasn't aware of what it might become. It was an infant wrapped in old clothes. The fact that it was a complicated moving image was so new, nobody knew what it meant.

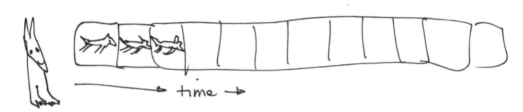

Now because it was new, and it was also a mechanical recording of images of reality, people weren't quite sure if it was an art form or just a record of the real world. This was the beginning of the debate in film theory about 'Realism' (representing the real) and 'constructivism' (film as a constructed set of images).

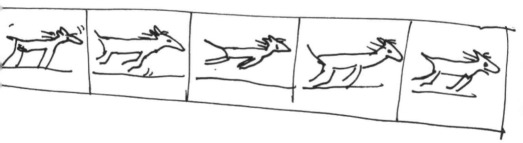

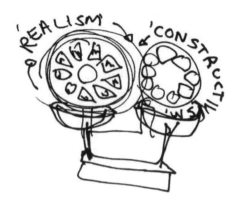

To begin with everyone compared film to older art forms, like painting and photography, and thought it might be inferior! Or they used film in ways that were based in the theatre, which is where films were shown initially.

It was a little while before people also began to think about stories.

Was film like a novel? Or was it in fact a completely new art-form all of its own, and, if so, what sort of art-form was it? Or was it, as some said, just entertainment?

# One basic question is 'What is a film?'

So what is a film?

You don't know do you?

Not really, but it seems obvious, a film is you know a film

MAN
It is a movie, or a documentary,
or a musical, or a bio-pic, or a
comedy, or a thriller, or a science-
fiction film, or a horror-thriller, or
a blaxpoitation movie, or an 'art-
work' - or a western, or a vampire
film, or a comedy-western-musical,
or a rom-com, or a bro-com.

RABBIT/DUCK
You don't know, do you?

MAN
Not really, but it seems obvious
- a film is, you know, a film.

RABBIT/DUCK
What it says in the dictionary is: a
story or event recorded by a camera
as a set of moving images and shown
in a cinema or on television.

MAN
There you go - it's obvious. A
story or an event on film.

RABBIT/DUCK
That might work as a general
definition but if we want to define
film we need to be more historically
and culturally specific, don't we?

Or, in other words, we need a theory of what film is, and what it
does - how film creates its own world and its ways of being
produced, distributed and watched. The fact that technology plays
such a big role in film also makes it a very radically different kind of
cultural structure and organization.

An American
might say

— what is a movie?

(and this word has interesting
American connotations)

It is almost as though..

An American might say "What is a movie?" (and this word has
interesting American connotations). It is almost as though a 'film' is
European and a 'movie' is American (and that difference goes quite
a long way).

A film is technically a motion picture, or set of images, which is
simply a series of still pictures shown very quickly so that they
simulate motion (which is the complicated bit). However a film/
movie can also be so much more than just those moving images -
it can tell a story, create beautiful images, tell political stories, or
even educate about difficult topics (like marriage/death or racism or
homosexuality).

So a film/movie can shock, entertain, provoke, annoy, or simply indulge people's desire for fantasy and escapism. Or it can tell a profound story in ways that challenge people's imagination. Of course most movies became commercial, told stories and entertained people - this became known as Hollywood (but how that grew is another story). Hollywood eventually came to dominate world cinema. How and why it did this is an important aspect of film theory.

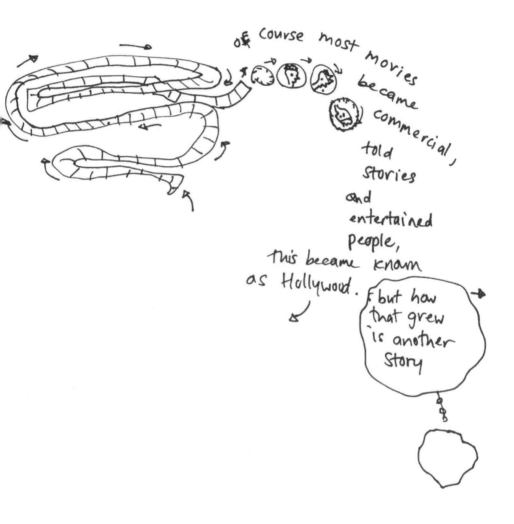

of course most movies became commercial, told stories and entertained people, this became known as Hollywood. but how that grew is another story

START.

FORM

CONTENT

STRUCTURE

Basically...

This is the beginning
of film theory debates

Classifying.

idea.

The camera directs
attention

Comedy stunts....

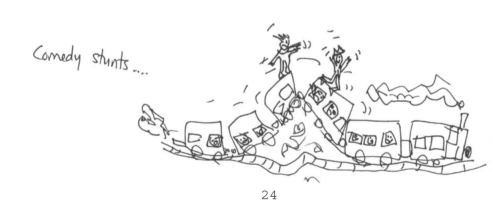

# Chapter 3 First theorists and Eisenstein

## Who was the first film theorist?

Well, probably the Lumière brothers were - and they had funny things to say about it. One of them famously said:

```
            LUMIÈRE BROTHER
        The cinema is an invention
        without a future.
```

This suggests that people can often get things wrong even when they are involved in it. The point about new inventions is that, at the time, no-one really sees what will evolve and what sort of consequences will flow from them. For the Lumière brothers to get it so wrong is really quite funny. (Someone else famously said that the horseless carriage (a car) was a silly idea and would never catch on - and someone once said football would never work on television!)

The Lumière brothers made lots of different kinds of short films but the excitement of just filming seemed to limit their thinking. Development didn't take long though. By 1903 an American by the name of Edwin S. Porter made a film with the gripping title of **The Life of an American Fireman** – which has a kind of story created through editing.

His even better **The Great Train Robbery** (1903) had it all: events, escapes and excitement – so this really is the first movie (or narrative film).

Actually making movies is rather different from theorizing about them and, although the Americans did a lot of innovating in terms of editing and narrative, it was the Europeans again who mostly did the thinking and writing (the Russians, Germans, French and Swedes).

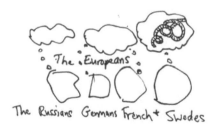

However, this starts another tradition, that of filmmakers who distrust theorizing about film, and pretty much think that film theory is unnecessary, as exemplified by this quote from a great contemporary filmmaker:

WERNER HERZOG
Academia is the death of cinema.
It is the very opposite of
passion. Film is not the art of
scholars, but of illiterates.

This conflict between theorists and makers has run and run, but there is no resolution because actually both have a place, and the theorizing of the Russians, such as Kuleshov and Eisenstein, had a direct effect on the way people made films.

# You can make a film without reading even one page of film theory!

# Lev Kuleshov

One of the earliest thinkers and practitoners was Lev Kuleshov – he was a pretty important early Russian guy. The first Kuleshov Workshop film, *The Extraordinary Adventures of Mr. West in the Land of the Bolsheviks,* hit theatres in 1924 - and was quite entertaining.

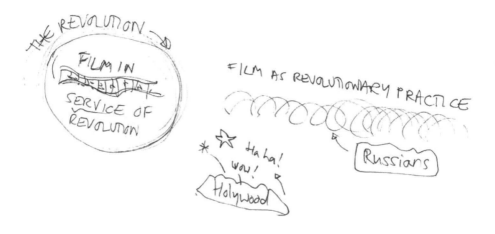

This was film tied to revolution, and of course the Russian Revolution was a pretty big deal in world politics. After overthrowing the Tsar and establishing communism in Russia, the new government pretty much decided that film, a new thing, should be in the service of the Revolution and would be great for mass propaganda. It is in this context that Russian filmmaking developed new ways of making films, and of theorizing about them. While Hollywood was perfecting the making of 'entertainment' films the Russians set about making film into a revolutionary practice. So their theory of film was all about how film could show, and manipulate, reality.

To this end there was a lot of experimentation and Lev Kuleshov was credited with inventing the 'Kuleshov Effect' (the trick of editing film in different ways).

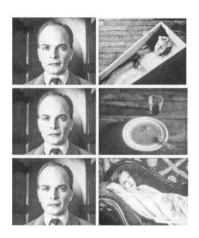

# Editing reality

Kuleshov famously edited together a short film in different ways in which a shot of the expressionless face of the Tsarist matinee idol Ivan Mosjoukine was alternated with various other shots (a girl in a coffin, a p[late of soup and a woman on a divan). This was the beginning of trick editing. The film was shown to an audience who then claimed that the expression on Mosjoukine's face was different each time he appeared, depending on whether he was looking at the plate of soup, the girl in the coffin, or the woman on the divan, and people thought he was showing an expression of hunger, grief or desire, respectively. In fact, of course, the footage of Mosjoukine was exactly the same shot each time. Pudovkin (who later claimed to have been the co-creator of the experiment) described in 1929 how the audience...

                    PUDOVKIN
          ... raved about the acting... the
          heavy pensiveness of his mood over
          the forgotten soup, were touched and
          moved by the deep sorrow with which he
          looked on the dead child, and noted
          the lust with which he observed the
          woman. But we knew that in all three
          cases the face was exactly the same.

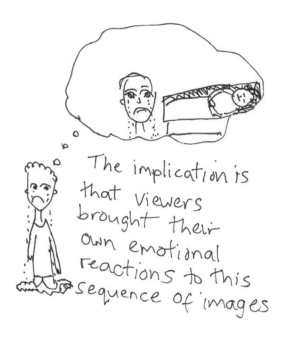

Kuleshov used this extraordinary experiment to show the importance and effectiveness of film editing. The conclusion he came to is that viewers actually brought their own emotional reactions to this sequence of images, and then attributed those reactions to the actor, investing their own feelings in the images. This may be a critical point in filmmaking thinking. Kuleshov believed this editing, along with montage, had to be the basis of cinema as an independent art form.

# Sergei Eisenstein (1898 - 1948)

The next most important Russian in terms of film theory and practice was Eisenstein. Everybody knows him for ***Battleship Potemkin***, ***October*** and ***Strike***. He did, of course, make other films but these three are the most important.

In a nutshell he is sometimes called the 'father of montage' – by which we mean he sort of invented it, which is a slight exaggeration, but he certainly put the theory unto paper and described all of the ways that 'montage' (or editing) could affect a film. Montage means putting images together in different ways - which obviously comes from Kuleshov, but Eisenstein took it all a lot further by theorizing all of the different ways that montage could be made to work. (Juxtaposition is another way of putting it.) According to Eisenstein's theory, the way that a film's aesthetic value could be judged was on its ability to transform the representation of reality and for him this was done through montage. Eisenstein argued that the collision between two adjoining images creates a third meaning (like the dialectic in theory). He said editing should make people think, not just see.

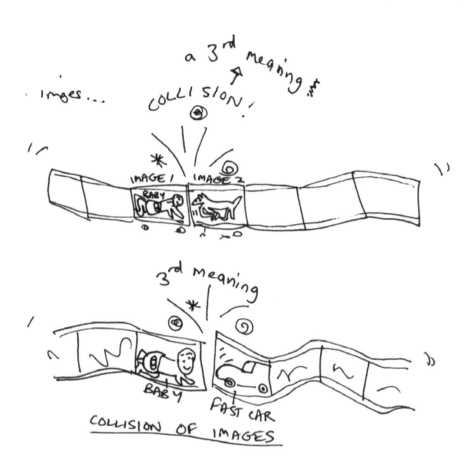

Eisenstein developed five kinds of montage.

- Metric
- Rhythmic
- Tonal
- Overtonal
- Intellectual

# Eisenstein and montage

This fundamental idea of playing with the sequence of images, and of juxtaposing things that would not normally be connected, made it possible to use film in radically new ways. So it is important to think about this in terms of the influence on film theory (and it is a quintessentially modernist technique).

# Metric

Sort of based in music –

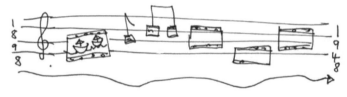

This was sort of based on music – like the metric beat – so it meant you composed film almost like music: the length of shots could influence the feel.

EISENSTEIN
The basic criterion is the absolute length of the shots. The shots are joined together according to their lengths in formula-scheme. This is realized in the repetition of these formulas.

33

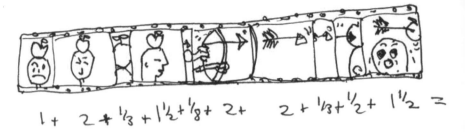

$$1 + 2 + \tfrac{1}{3} + 1\tfrac{1}{2} + \tfrac{1}{8} + 2 + \quad 2 + \tfrac{1}{3} + \tfrac{1}{2} + 1\tfrac{1}{2} =$$

He was simply using the timing of the shots to create effects (rather than naturalistic forms). Tension is obtained by the effect of mechanical acceleration by shortening the pieces while preserving the original proportions of the formula. This technique produces a quantitative effect that can be reduced to a mathematical formula (Eisenstein really wanted to produce a 'scientific' theory of how to make films).

# Rhythmic

This is rather like music theory in that the use of the shots builds up a feeling, an audience response, or a mood, that can be very effective.

Basically this relates to the famous steps sequence in the film *Battleship Potemkin* - where the shots of moving feet and people are inter-cut in ways that powerfully build an unbearable tension. This was a wholly new filmic technique that has been hugely influential.

'THE 'DESCENT' OF THE PRAM'. THE FEET BECOMES THE 'ROLLING DOWN'

Eisenstein explains:

EISENSTEIN
The 'drumbeat' of the soldiers' feet
descending the steps destroys all
metrical conventions. It occurs outside
the intervals prescribed by the metre
and each time it appears in a different
shot resolution. The final build-up of
tension is produced by swiching from
the rhythm of the solders' tread as
they descend the steps to another, new
form of movement - the next stage in
the intensification of the same action
- the pram rolling down the steps.
Here the pram works in relation to the
feet as a direct staged accelerator.
The 'descent' of the feet becomes
the 'rolling down' of the pram.

# Tonal

What Eisenstein means by tonal montage is basically the setting of
the tone - or the construction of a mood - in the film. In other words,
the emotional tone of a sequence directs this kind of montage.
When portraying people falling in love the edit cuts to flying birds
or moonlight or other images that reinforce the tone, which is often
backed up by music. (To put it crudely – and sound later becomes
very important.)

This characteristic of the shot can be
measured precisely. It is constructed
on the dominant emotional resonance of
the shot. If we designate the shot as
a more gloomy, we can play with
lighting and use specific degree of the
illumination to get this effect. It is
light tonality.

As an example Eisenstein put the fog in the Odessa Port sequence in
**Battleship Potemkin** all over the place. This helped to reinforce the
'tone' of the film.

## Overtonal

Overtonal montage is a combination of all the three types of
montage discussed above. (Over-the-top montage?) Overtonal
montage demands that more than one type of montage occur
together, thereby creating a film effect in which the methods exist
in a relationship and may even be in conflict with one another.
Eisenstein talks about the editing of a sequence in which a group
of people are setting off into the sea in small boats on a gloomy

morning. Through editing the audience is made aware that the force of the ocean, much more powerful than the boats, is likely to act on them. First there are the shots which show very small boats on a large expanse of water with a gloomy sky. This is followed by clever edits from person to person, from boat to boat using the waves of the ocean as guides. Then there follows a lengthy shot of stormy clouds gathering in the sky, the ocean itself is shown as immense and there are long shots of the people in the boats. Overall this shows the powerlessness of the people against the 'force of nature' and makes the audience worry about what will happen to the people on the boats. So again the editing builds the filmic effect through a complex manipulation of individual shots.

If you think about it this a key aspect of filmmaking, creating the tone of a film. All of these types of montage are also really early theories of how to edit film. The outcome may be different from what Eisenstein claimed but the tricks of editing were radical and revolutionary, and changed film for ever.

# Intellectual

In this elaborate theory of filmmaking Eisenstein then moved on to intellectual montage – which he saw as the highest category of montage. (We could call it 'ideas montage', or the things that pop into the mind when things are juxtaposed.)

Eisenstein argued that intellectual montage was a montage of overtones of an intellectual order (or about the conflict between intellectual effects). A combination of shots give us an abstract image and there is no need to explain it – the ideas are created by the intellectual montage - this is the conscious creation of new ideas when two shots or images are cut together to form a new idea or object.

If you think about the first time anyone filmed a depressed looking person on a bridge, staring at the water you sort of get the idea. (Montage can become cliché?)

Actually Eisenstein didn't just talk about montage and editing, he talked about most aspects of film and film theory, which is why he is still so important. He set out to create a complete theory of film right from the off, and in the heat of the Russian revolution.

STILL
IMPORTANT

A close up view:

long-shot' film theory
'medium-shot' film theory
'close-up' film theory

In a later essay he wrote in 1945 called **'A Close up View'** he talked about the different kinds of approaches to film theory and came up with a useful distinction.

He said you have 'long-shot' film theory which looks at the broader questions of the social and political impact of film – the socio-political mode of film analysis. 'Medium-shot' film theory looks at the human interactions, stories and everyday feel of film, which is what film critics tend to discuss, as in "Was it a good story?' 'Close-up' film theory, he said, breaks the film down into its constituent parts and examines each aspect in detail. He used the phrase "resolves the film into its elements", which quite clearly sounds like formalist film theory, and almost like the Semiotics and close analysis of contemporary film theory.

This scenario rather clearly pinpoints the fact that there are quite different ways of thinking about film, something we will keep coming back to.

different ways of thinking

One underrated but quite interesting film theorist from the early days was Vachel Lindsey, a practising poet who decided he also knew about film. His ***The Art of the Moving Picture (1915)*** is a brave and quite prescient discussion about how film worked and its relationship with older forms of culture. He called films 'photoplays', which in itself is interesting, and he talked about the important different types of 'photoplay' (interesting because it links to the theatre):

- The photoplay of action (precursor of the action movie)
- The intimate photoplay (the love story)
- The motion picture of splendor (the blockbuster)

Here you have the basic categories of Hollywood, followed by a clever discussion of how film was a radical new cultural form and should probably evolve away from the theatre. He also talks about film as a language and this points directly to later forms of film criticism and Semiotics.

Not bad for someone who didn't grace the halls of academe.

STANLEY KAUFFMANN
In the field of film aesthetics, it is the first important American work, still important - *The Art of the Moving Picture* is astonishing.

40

So the question with Eisenstein and his film theory is precisely whether he is still important and relevant, other than in the sense that everyone uses complex editing as part of their filmic craft, which is a sign of his influence.

One critic had this to say:

DAVID THOMSON
With Eisenstein, you confront a demonic, baroque visual theatricality, helplessly adhering to the confused theories of his writing on film. And he was quickly in decline... There are those who still acclaim him, but his influence is now very hard to detect.

That may seem harsh but it may not be that untrue. Eisenstein belonged to a radical Marxist tradition that saw everything in fairly black and white terms. That era has long since passed and is quite discredited. Film has now developed in many different ways. Eisenstein contributed to the theory of film, but then so did D.W. Griffith, the crazy American racist. The dialectic of history is a funny thing when you look at it, and the truth can be edited in many different ways. So it is oddly fitting that Eisenstein and Griffith are both sort of revered and sort of ignored in equal measure.

It might be funny to think of a film script where Eisenstein and Griffith argued about film together and tried to come to an agreement on film theory. It would probably end with extreme violence and cutting shots from one corpse to the other – a very postmodern movie.

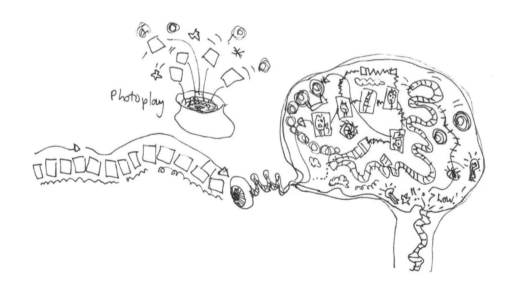

Photoplay

# Chapter 4 Münsterberg and Balázs

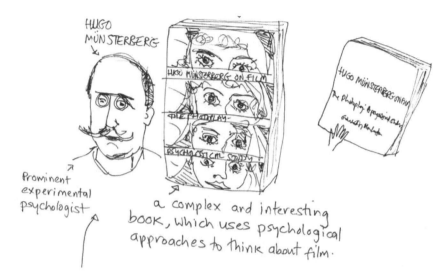

HUGO MÜNSTERBERG

Prominent experimental psychologist

a complex and interesting book, which uses psychological approaches to think about film.

Now often regarded as the first serious work of film theory, the relatively obscure Hugo Münsterberg's *The Photoplay: A Psychological Study (1916)*, is a complex and interesting book, which uses psychological approaches to think about film. It was written by a German who, although being one of the most prominent experimental psychologists alive at the time (1916), was almost entirely ignored by the wider film world until the 1970s when his work was re-discovered. The fact that he died just after he wrote the work may have had something to do with this, and the fact that the work wasn't in print. He was a Professor of Pyschology at Harvard University, no less, and was influential in what we might call applied psychology, and his interest in film was a personal, perhaps unusual one.

His work is interesting because he, like Lindsey, thinks about moving images (a film) as a 'photoplay' and compares film to a stage play. So he is immediately thinking about the difference between films and the theatre. His work is especially interesting because of its claim to an affinity between the techniques of cinema and the mechanisms of the mind. This is a radical idea that picks up on the potential psychological implications of the way that projected moving images impact on the spectator. (Can our minds be altered by film watching?) This is very different from his precursor Lindsey.

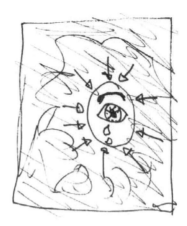

Unlike other theorists who have argued that what is unique to cinema is its ability to clearly depict reality, Münsterberg surprisingly claims that the photoplay in fact shapes the reality it presents according to the laws of thought, rather than, as often argued,

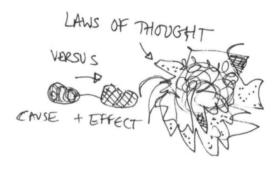

according to the laws of cause and effect, or of technology. For example, he argues that the photoplay (film) is able to mirror the mental act of attention, that it tends to isolate and focus upon some element of experience, or idea, in such a way that other elements fade from focus and become less vivid (almost like meditation). So for him this new medium, film, mimics the way the mind works rather than projects reality. This is a very radical idea that has implications for much later film theory.

Ironically Münsterberg was just about to give a lecture at Harvard when he suffered a massive heart attack at the podium and died - quite a way for an academic to go out. It is like the melodramatic ending of a very bad film. The good bit is that Münsterberg prefigures the recent rise in cognitive film theory.

# Bela Balázs (1884–1949)

Someone else we need to talk about in the development of film theory is this very interesting Hungarian poet, screenwriter, playwright, film critic, director, and also the author of the libretto for Béla Bartók's famous *Bluebeard's Castle* (1912). His pen name was Bela Balázs but his real name was a slightly more pedestrian Herbert Bauer. It is slightly difficult to place him as some of his very early work influenced Eisenstein and company. but his later work wasn't re-discovered until the 1960s. He was also a revolutionary and a believer in the artistic merit of silent film. Balázs is often considered as the main theorist of silent cinema, physiognomy (the way people look) and of the close-up. So he was interested in the idea that film brought back a visual culture which he claimed had been lost in a word-based, literary culture – a radically interesting idea. His philosophical ideas about film are still being incorporated into the main debates.

the Close up

Balázs's key idea is that the...

... most subjective and individual of
human manifestations is rendered
objective in the close-up.

BALÁZS (CONT'D)
Film takes you closer to a star than
any ordinary human contact ever would.

Balázs emphasized in his early writing that the moving pictures
brought back the language of the body and of the expressions of
the human face, in close up, which he argued "had been buried by
the culture of books and words. "

BALÁZS
Facial expression is the most
subjective manifestation of man,
more subjective than speech.

Balázs wrote in *Theory of the Film:*

BALÁZS
The language of the face cannot
be suppressed or controlled.

The close-up was therefore for Balázs the most important feature of
film art, which made it different from all other arts, especially from
the theatre, which was more gestural.

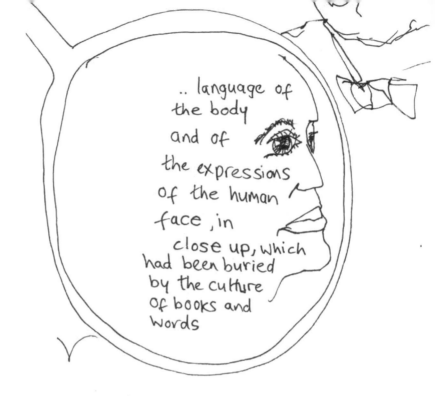

.. language of
the body
and of
the expressions
of the human
face, in
close up, which
had been buried
by the culture
of books and
words

BALÁZS
Pan in on me and you'll see
something that will surprise you!

His **Theory of the Film** (1952), which was first published in Moscow in 1945 as **The Art of Cinema**, has become quite influential. In it Balázs developed his earlier ideas and used writings he had developed at the State Film Institute.

His history is complicated and it was in 1922 that he started writing on film, publishing film reviews for the Vienna daily newspaper **Der Tag**. Two years later he would release the first film theory book ever written in German, **Der Sichtbare Mensch**. In this book he started to sketch out his ideas on the aesthetic and cultural position of silent cinema, particularly in relation to the 'traditional' arts such as theatre, literature and painting. His discussions about film as an art clearly influenced Brecht, Eisenstein, Kracauer and others, and he is still being rediscovered.

The close up makes film more emotional
than anyone could have thought of!

Balázs also discussed the idea that film was a 'universal language' which had radical potentiality, and this is also something film theory keeps coming back to. (Can film talk more easily to everyone than the written word? - a question that 'Third Cinema' has raised.) He was therefore proposing a truly radical outlook for film that could transform popular culture. Many of these ideas were taken up much later in the 1960s and '70s.

# Chapter 5 Freud and film (Expressionism)

STUDENT
Why do we need to talk about
Freud in relation to film?

PROFESSOR
Because he transformed the way that we
think about individuals and their way
of living in society, and in particular
how we understood art and culture!

STUDENT
But what in relation to film?

PROFESSOR
Well, two key things; first Freud
said that dreams were the royal
road to the unconscious, and also
that emotions and feelings are
linked to the unconscious, which
can be triggered by art. It is this
connection we are interested in.

STUDENT
So?

PROFESSOR
Well put simply, films are quite often
like dreams and so in a strange way
they can make us feel things we didn't
really know we were reacting too.

STUDENT
No idea what you are talking about,
I just want to know about the sex.

PROFESSOR
Well indeed, that's what Freud
said, we have sex on the brain.

well..

STUDENT
Well that's not exactly a
revelation is it, any 16 year
old could tell you that.

Ironically, what Freud was talking about in psychoanalysis was in part about sex, but also about a much more complicated process in which an individual becomes a member of society by the repression of many elements of sexuality, and of defining themselves in relation to a social order in which sexuality is often taboo.

This repression produces the unconscious and leads to ways in which communication is often not about the obvious, surface ideas but about deeper, stranger things.

These ideas heavily influenced the Expressionists and the Surrealists and led to ways of thinking about how film communicates meaning.

# Psychoanalysis and film were made for each other.

```
          FREUD
The conscious mind may be compared to
a fountain playing in the sun and
falling back into the great
subterranean pool of subconscious from
which it rises.
```

The discovery of the 'Unconscious' and the realization that man, and woman, did not act as rational beings, but were pushed this way and that by drives, powerful repressed emotions and tendencies, led to a sea-change in culture and film.

Film can brilliantly convey the unspoken menace, the uncanny and the repressed emotions of individuals. This was brilliantly developed by the Expressionists and to a lesser extent the Surrealists (See **Freud for Beginners**). The **Cabinet of Dr Caligari** is, in part, an essay on the importance of psychoanalysis in film.

The aptly named Mr. Fearing said this of film and Freud:

MR. FEARING
Analysis of film content assumes two levels of meaning, one of which is manifest and one of which is hidden. The last carries the "real" meaning for the mass audience. This audience is presumed to intuit or in some manner become aware of the motifs in **the film which satisfy and express its** hidden needs. This seems to mean that the 'unconscious' intuitions of the **makers of films communicate to the** 'unconscious' minds of the mass audience. (Fearing, 1948).

The hidden depths of film show us the neurotic in society, the sociopath, the damaged individual and how trauma from childhood always haunts the adult. Hitchcock's **Psycho** is theory in action. Repression occurs when the individual locks traumatic memories inside - and film can unlock them.

Freud's idea of the Unconscious is one of the dominant ideologies expressed in the horror film – the idea of secret desires that lie hidden from the conscious mind but drive our motivations. Vampire films encompass sexual repression, desire, fear and the sense of the uncanny in a wonderful combination.

So Freud says that the trauma —

ow!

argh!

Freud says that the trauma experienced during childhood can be a leading cause of mental illness in the adult. Repression is a central fact of life in a civilized society, and repression leads to reaction, which emerges not only in action, but in language (the Freudian slip).

neurotic behaviour
"it prevails"

In many films, neurotic behavior is prevalent in the 'villains', with strangely heightened and dangerous sexual awareness in the 'heroine'. In the symbols of dream images, and the unconscious desires expressed in dreams, there is another key element of Freud's theories which is relevant to film theory.

COCKS

The similarity between dreaming and watching a film has been noted. Aapart from the coincidence of their birth and their intercourse with dreams, however, psychoanalysis and film also share certain important characteristics. Both are artifacts of the scientific and industrial age. Both are concerned with what the mind sees. Both treat time as highly malleable and the unconscious as timeless. Both are concerned with tangible reality – psychological and photographic – but both are also vitally concerned with the intangible.

Scientific
+
industrial
age

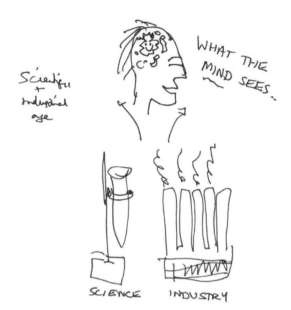

WHAT THE
MIND SEES..

SCIENCE          INDUSTRY

Unconscious and timeless

# German Expressionism (1920s and '30s)

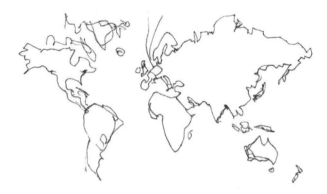

Making psychologically radical films in a radical era. The world of light and dark.

Everybody was making films, in many parts of the world, and interestingly many of the older films have disappeared, so we don't know the history exactly. However, in terms of film theory and film practice, it is pretty much agreed that the Germans succeeded the Russians in terms of producing the most interesting and influential ideas. The arts movement that became known as German Expressionism grew out of a group of like-minded artists who all rejected the traditional forms and practices of art and wanted to find new ways of representing reality. A bunch of artists got

1905

A bunch of artists..
got tsadn in Dresden-

together in 1905 in Dresden and called themselves Die Brücke (The Bridge), and Kadinsky joined them later. The journal *Der Sturm* became the focus of their theoretical discussion and it was in this journal that the term 'Expressionism' was first used.

Rather then being scientific these artists were more interested in the inner life and were influenced by the theories of Sigmund Freud.

Expressionism is the movement in the fine arts that emphasized the expression of one's inner self and personal angst rather than solely being realistic about the world and life.

We can say that Freud, fear and the fantastic are pretty much the basics of German Expressionism. For film theory it is as much a question of how the spectator relates unconsciously to the ideas of film, as it is to the manifest content of film. This is sometimes called discussing spectatorship.

Germany in the 1920s and '30s was in a state of turmoil. There was economic crisis, threats of revolution, radical politics and then the rise of fascism. The Weimar Republic was a fascinating time in which artistic expression was highly strung, highly developed and very political.

Expressionism can be seen as a reaction to modern science, logic and technical rationalism. Its classical work was marked by aesthetic intensity, a wilful divergence from previous modes of thinking, a tendency to short forms of expression as a way of concentrating and condensing, and an acute self-consciousness about the limits of language, using imagery more often. The all time great film from this period is **The Cabinet of Dr Caligari**, still a shocking film to watch in terms of style, form and impact. Movies from this era, like **Metropolis,** are also important.

Expressionism started out as a movement in painting and sculpture but it quickly spread to the fledgling movie industry in Europe. The majority of film expressionists came from Germany, so the term German Expressionism became popular when describing this movement in film. However there were many other filmmakers who deployed expressionist themes but who were not German.

Dr Caligari

Norbert Lynton summed up Expressionism pretty well:

NORBERT LYNTON

All human action is expressive; a
gesture is an intentionally expressive
action. All art is expressive - of its
author and of the situation in which
he works - but some art is intended to
move us through visual gestures that
transmit, and perhaps give release
to, emotions and emotionally charged
messages. Such art is expressionist.

Part of the reason the expressionist movement flourished in
Germany was because whilst the demand for film was on the rise the
import of foreign films had been banned. So a hard-up, artistically
inclined industry needed to be inventive. That is why some critics
argue that the non-realistic, geometrically absurd art direction
was actually born out of necessity. The basic line is that early
expressionist films lacked budgets and time, so the filmmakers were
forced to play around with lighting, shadows and cheap minimalist
sets. (Not a very convincing argument.)

They came up with the idea of making the sets part of the action. They were more like paintings than realistic backgrounds. Initially, the sets were highly symbolic, stylized and non-realistic , sometimes geometric, and they were filmed indoors.

NOSFERATU

The films presented dark human experiences – madness, betrayal, paranoia and obsession (*Nosferatu, 1922*). The point of view of such films was generally subjective (inner moods, feelings, perceptions). The effect was extreme moodiness. The extreme camera angles often suggest being watched - something Hitchcock borrowed later. The ideas of psychoanalysis clearly influenced many of these films. In *The Cabinet of Dr Caligari* some of the action is in a mental asylum.

# Key elements of expressionist films

- Basic re-writing of reality in filmmaking.

- Emphasis on design or mise-en-scène, uncanny atmosphere and composition (sets). Films evoke mystery, extremity, alienation, disharmony, hallucination, dreams, and destabilization of the 'ordinary'.

- These films often blur the boundary between reality and dreams.

- They tend to be fatalistic.

- There are common images such as stairs, empty hallways and corridors. The use of harsh contrasts of light and dark (chiaroscuro) reflect and express disturbed psyches and an oppressive world.

- Voice-overs are common.

- Distortion is created by the use of make-up, strange camera angles, costumes, strange sets, and the actors' body language.

- Classic examples: *The Cabinet of Dr. Caligari, Nosferatu, The Last Laugh, Metropolis, M, The Golem.*

Fairly obviously, expressionist modes of portraying a darker world hugely influenced later horror films, Film Noir and many other psychological genres.

A rather different strand...

rotten...

Everything was in chaos and the old,

# Chapter 6 Surrealism

Another related, but rather different, strand of thinking in European culture that emerged in the 1920s, and which also influenced film-theory and filmmaking, was Surrealism.

You need to throw your mind back (to use a surrealist notion) to what the world was like after the 1st World War. Everything was in chaos and the old, bourgeois order seemed rotten and dishonest. Dada and Surrealism were artistic reactions to this sense of disorder, decline and dishonesty.

Dadaism was a movement that was a protest against everything. It was opposed to a world that seemed nonsensical, absurd and corrupt, which was characterized by the slaughter and stupidity of the war -- a war seemingly fought over nothing but which killed millions of people. Artists reacted very strongly to the insanity of the war – and sought new artistic means of thinking about the world.

Dada itself was a made up, nonsensical word, but the aim was to expose the craziness of the world and the way that things were organized. Artists like Duchamp and other leading exponents of Dada did things like make nonsensical speeches or construct poems at random, with the now famous 'cutting up words from newspaper articles and picking them out of a sack' technique.

Duchamp exhibited what he called 'found objects' out of context, like his famous Urinal. This was to say that there was no meaning in the world anymore and that rationality was a fiction. These ideas re-emerged in movie-making in the 1960s in the work of people like Roeg, Lynch and Fellini.

# The origins of Surrealism

Surrealism was founded as a movement by the artist/theorist André Breton in 1924. It was more organized and politically revolutionary than Dada, which was simply against everything. The Surrealists produced a manifesto and declared themselves to be the enemies of bourgeois society.

Many of the Surrealists were Marxists who were determined to transform society and who also had a rather old-fashioned romantic faith in the power of art. This was combined with a major interest in the ideas of good old Sigmund Freud, the father of psychoanalysis. The Surrealist Manifesto has been widely regarded as the foremost essential guide to comprehending Surrealism as a movement - and is still widely read.

drawing on

Breton, drawing on the ideas of psychoanalysis and the unconscious, talked of "pure psychic automatism" and of his belief in the "omnipotence of dreams in the undirected play of thought". Many of the surrealist artists were also influenced by the ideas of the 'untutored' art of children, of madness and of so called 'primitive art forms'. Their art work used and reflected these techniques, using shocking, irrational, or absurd imagery and Freudian dream symbolism to challenge the traditional function of art to represent reality. Surrealist cinema is characterised by unexpected juxtapositions, a frequent use of shocking imagery, and a sense of absurdity. One of the surrealist terms was that of 'fishing in the unconscious', which rather neatly sums it up.

In some ways surrealist theory has entered the mainstream and surrealist ideas are everywhere. Salvador Dali has become the Liberace of the art world.

The classic surrealist film was made in 1928 by novice director Luis Buñuel., who was a Spanish film enthusiast and a modernist poet. Working with Salvador Dali, he made *Un Chien Andalou (An Andalusian Dog)*. The basic story seems to be about a quarrel between two lovers, but the time scheme and the logic are impossible. Odd titles announce meaningless intervals of time passing, as when "sixteen years earlier" appears within an action that continues without pause.

There is a series of shocking sequences which were designed to challenge any audience: a hand opens to reveal a wound from which a group of ants emerges and a young man drags two grand pianos across a room, laden with a pair of dead donkeys and two old priests, in a vain attempt to win the amour of a woman he openly lusts after. The impact is still shocking today; the impact back then must have been electric. These are just two of the more bizarre sequences in the film; the most famous scene occurs near the beginning, when Buñuel himself is seen sharpening a razor on a balcony and then ritualistically slitting the eyeball of a young woman who sits passively in a chair a moment later. Nobody forgets that image.

The connections between things are not taken for granted and are in fact postulated as being anti-rational; that is the essence of Surrealism. Fish and films are brought together to show up good old bourgeois rationality.

SALVADOR DALÍ
Surrealism is destructive, but it destroys only what it considers to be shackles limiting our vision.

Film theory then was clearly in some senses lagging behind what people actually did in terms of experimentation, montage, Surrealism and critical and innovative films. In some ways film theory wasn't even seen as important until after the 2$^{nd}$ World War. Since the rise of film theory in the 1970s however people have often revisited what went on earlier to look for clues about how it developed.

# Chapter 7 Bergson and Kracauer

Another writer who got rediscovered in thinking about film theory was Henri Bergson, the philosopher (it is interesting to think about how and why people have started to re-write film history and theory).

Anyway, this French philosopher Henri Bergson wrote some stuff called **Matter and Memory** which is now seen, by some people, as anticipating the development of film theory at the very time that the cinema was just being born as a new medium - the early 1900s. In it he talked about the need for new ways of thinking about movement in general, and developed the terms 'the movement-image' and 'the time-image'. Frankly, these ideas weren't particularly linked to thinking directly about film, and there are reasons to think that Bergson didn't even like film when he saw it. In particular, in his 1906 essay **L'illusion Cinématographique** he actually says he rejects film as an example of what he had in mind when talking about the movement-image.  This is all a bit odd, but the point is that Bergson did start to think about how we relate to the moving image – which is, of course, an important issue in film theory.

At one point Bergson likens the process he discusses to the mind and the image to the cinema apparatus. He argues that the camera begins with a real movement, then breaks it down mechanically into what is a series of static single frames and then it returns the movement through the projecting apparatus into the finished product. So in the end the movement that we see is a reconstituted illusion.

He argues that the camera begins with a real movement, then breaks it down mechanically into what is a series of static single frames and

Dolly →

1s →

and then it returns the movement through the projecting apparatus into the finished product →

This is exactly what a film is, so in a way Bergson is getting at a difficult question.

# What is the relationship of the mind to the way that the cinema works?

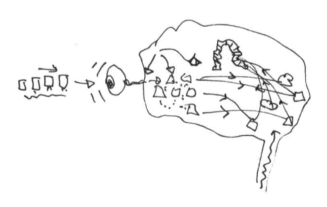

This seriously is the Big Question of Film Theory!

Such is the contrivance of the cinematograph. And such is also that of our knowledge

Despite Bergson being a bit sniffy... about film back then – he has been re-discovered and in particular Giles Deleuze → the French philosopher developed his ideas in his Cinéma 1 and Cinéma II (1983 – 1985),

... and he took **Matter and Memory** as the basis of his philosophy of film and revisited Bergson's concepts, also combining them with the semiotics of Charles Sanders Peirce. An interesting mix that we will come back to.

Giles Deleuze

(first film theorist
'sans moustache'?)

stubble

Again this hints at the idea that film and memory/thinking have a close relationship, an idea that was to become quite important.

# Another European interlude

As we said before, the Americans tended to make the films, and the money, and the Europeans tended to think about the films, and the money. So here we will look at some relevant European film theorists.

Several have been 'rediscovered' in later years, so it is slightly difficult to assess their importance, but at least they had interesting things to say about film theory (and remember film theory is not the same as criticism or history).

Siegfried Kracauer, around at the same time as Walter Benjamin, and very loosely associated with the Frankfurt School, a group of German Marxist cultural theorists, wrote quite extensively on film. Like Benjamin he could be a little obtuse, and sometimes even annoying in his academic insistence on elaborate theories, but he also had a strong political viewpoint based on his reactions to Nazi Germany. Some people argue that he is very important in the development of film theory, whilst other people argue that he is a bit incomprehensible and prone to elaborate theories. The film jury is still out.

STUDENT
How can there be such total disagreement about somebody? It doesn't make sense, either he is a good film theorist or he isn't.

PROFESSOR
Well the trouble is, maybe he is both at the same time, in that he says lots of interesting things about film, but maybe gets the main arguments wrong. Some people say Kracauer was one of two most important film critics of the Weimar Republic, as well as one of the most influential people in the development of critical film theory, particularly in relation to aesthetics.

STUDENT
So what did he write?

PROFESSOR
Well, in 1927 he produced a strange essay called **The Ornament of the Masses,** which was an attack on Hollywood and mass culture. He went on about the Tiller girls and the petty-bourgeois audiences who watched them. This early stuff was a fairly sociological analysis of the role that film played in the new popular culture of the 1930s during the rise of fascism in Europe. Then right through to his **Theory of Film: The Redemption of Physical Reality (1960)** he produced a lot of ideas about what film should be, although he seemingly in the end just argued that 'Realism' was the main function of film.

Much too complex philosophical position

Naïve realism...

Kracauer is accused of simultaneously having a much too complex philosophical position about the nature of film and of advocating a 'naïve Realism'. He talked about how the cinema is "animated by a desire to picture transient material life." In other words, "nature caught in the act." To him filming 'real stuff' was better than making things up, which does seem a rather basic idea. However as a critic of authoritarian aesthetics, he argued that cinema should focus on the unpredictable, unplanned events of everyday existence.

Realism...

Nature caught in the act

KRACAUER

Films are true to the medium to the extent that they penetrate the world before our eyes.

Somebody said about his book:

ANONYMOUS

On the contrary, much as *Theory of Film* strives toward systematicity and transparency, the text remains uneven, opaque, and contradictory

ANONYMOUS (CONT'D)
in many places, defying the
attempt to deduce from it any
coherent, singular position.

This isn't very helpful other than to suggest that he brings a philosophical, sociological and contradictory argument to bear on thinking about film.

What Kracauer does do is to attempt to think about film aesthetics and to develop a full philosophical description of the nature of film. He probably failed badly but it was an important starting point! He also tried to formally show how film created reality, which is a pretty key question.

We can argue that the most difficult aspects of his **Theory of Film** are his notion of reality as 'physical' or 'visible' reality, his argument that film is an extension of the 'photographic approach' and ultimately that 'films come into their own when they record and reveal physical reality.' This is what people mean by naïve Realism. Some documentary filmmakers like this sort of argument but it really just ignores the 'made-up' nature of film (which is a created medium).

Here is a great quote that sums things up in relation to Mr Kracauer:

PAULINE KAEL
There are men whose concept of love is
so boring and nagging that you decide
if that's what love is you don't
want it, you want something else.
That's how I feel about Kracauer's
'cinema'. I want something else.

STUDENT
That claim that film is an extension
of photography is pretty dumb really
isn't it, because film is moving image
and photography isn't - that is what
you call a great big difference.

PROFESSOR
Bazingah!

# Chapter 8 Brecht, Benjamin and film

Another German who contributed a great deal to theories of film and theatre was the inimitable Bertolt Brecht: poet, critic, playwright and general all-round cultural theorist.

STUDENT
Who was Brecht and why is he important to film theory? I thought he was a poet.

PROFESSOR
Well indeed he was a poet, but he was also a playwright, theorist, cultural agitator, communist and global disturber of bourgeois prejudices.

STUDENT
Did he make films?

PROFESSOR
Well, not a lot, but his theories about theatre, Realism and new approaches were hugely influential in film theory, and filmmaking.

STUDENT
So who was he then, and what's the USP?

PROFESSOR

Well Bertolt Brecht was born on
10th February 1898 in Augsburg,
Germany and became one of the
country's most influential poets,
playwrights and screenwriters
during the 1920s and 1930s.

His best known work internationally
was the musical *The Threepenny Opera*
(written with Kurt Weill), which also
produced a hit-song *Mac the Knife*,
but his plays such as *Mother Courage
and Her Children* or *The Good Person
of Szechwan* were equally important.

STUDENT

Why exactly?

PROFESSOR

Because they revolutionized the way
theatre was presented, attacked the
old fashioned 'realism' of plays and
stirred everybody up!

# Brecht's big idea

One of Brecht's most important ideas was what he called the 'defamiliarization effect' or the 'estrangement effect', which is often mistranslated as the 'alienation effect'. What it meant was that you confronted the audience with the fact that the work of art was a made-up illusion; you showed them that this was an illusion in progress. Brecht described this as:

> BRECHT
> Stripping the event of its self-evident, familiar, obvious quality and creating a sense of astonishment and curiosity about them.

He used various new theatrical techniques, some of which he invented, such as the actor speaking directly to the audience, or very harsh stage lighting to avoid illusion, and even the use of songs to interrupt the stage action. It was a case of anything to break up the normal way of doing stuff in the theatre. In addition to this Brecht had tricks like using placards and even making the actors recite the stage directions out loud during the play itself (this is anti-Realism).

Brecht basically had nothing but complete disdain for the conventional, commercial 'bourgeois' theatre/film of his time. He thought it was like a "branch of the narcotics business."

STUDENT
That's a bit left field isn't it?

PROFESSOR
Well it sort of was back then, but now it seems obvious - and attacking films and theatre that are just entertainment and emotional manipulation was also a fairly common idea in the 1920s and 30s. Left wing critics, poets, modernists and painters all attacked the idea of 'bourgeois Realism'. Brecht drew things together and came up with a complete theory, which is why he is so important.

STUDENT
Yes, but what about film?

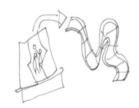

PROFESSOR
We are just coming to that. First you have to understand two things: One, film really develops out of theatre, two, the emotional manipulation of the audience through identification was a key characteristic of both.

PROFESSOR (CONT'D)
So Brecht's revamping of theatre led
to a change in film theory as well.

STUDENT
And how exactly does that
manifest itself then.

PROFESSOR
Well in addition to the theatre,
Brechtian theories and techniques
have had a big influence over certain
strands of film theory and cinematic
practice. Brecht's influence can
clearly be detected in the films of
Jean-Luc Godard, Luis Buñuel, Lindsay
Anderson, Rainer Werner Fassbinder,
Joseph Losey, Nagisa Oshima, Ritwik
Ghatak, Lars von Trier, Jan Bucquoy
and Hal Hartley, just to name a few.

STUDENT
That's a lot of important filmmakers.

PROFESSOR
Exactly. The influence of his ideas
has been immense, and is still
being felt. He shook up the idea
of making films that were either
realistic, naturalistic, or just plain
entertainment. His ideas led to a
theory of filmmaking that highlighted
the way that film was actually
constructed. So, as in the theatre,
the idea was to look at what we're
actually doing making a film - let's
make the audience part of the film.

STUDENT
There's a film about
Brecht, isn't there?

# Walter Benjamin, film and technology

Walter Benjamin, friend of Brecht and Marxist theorist/philosopher of culture writing in the 1930s, somewhat transformed the debate about the cultural impact of moving images, and of culture in general, when he wrote the now famous (infamous) article *The Mechanical Work of Art in the Age of Reproduction* (1936). His work is notoriously difficult and rather complex - at one point he said that everything has 36 levels of meaning! However in respect of film theory he was clear that it was an important new medium and that it could have a major impact on the way that people perceive the world. He talked about how the audience for film watched it in a state of 'distraction' rather than, as it were, concentration.

STUDENT
How come if you deliberately
go to the movies you are being
'distracted'? I don't get it.

PROFESSOR
Well, it is a little difficult but
what Benjamin seems to be saying
is that it is such a new kind of
experience that it inevitably changes
the nature of how people engage.
Watching a film is totally different
from reading a book, for example.

BENJAMIN
Reception in a state of distraction,
which is increasing noticeably in all
fields of art and is symptomatic of
profound changes in apperception, finds
in the film its true means of exercise.

**Benjamin's next slightly complicated idea is summed up in this quote:**

```
              BENJAMIN (CONT'D)
The camera introduces us to unconscious
optics as does psychoanalysis
to unconscious impulses.
```

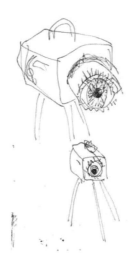

```
              STUDENT
What the hell does that mean?
```

```
              PROFESSOR
Well, I think he is saying that the
camera shows us a kind of reality that
is not perceptible to the normal eye,
because it slows down and exposes
reality (kind of freezes it) which
changes our unconscious ability to see
the world in a particular way - that is
what he means by 'unconscious optics'.
```

```
              STUDENT
Way to go, but what about
the psychoanalysis bit?
What does that mean?
```

PROFESSOR

Well as you know psychoanalysis
showed us how to think about the
reality of unconscious impulses
and drives. It brought them out
into the open, and Benjamin is
saying that film does the same
thing; it brings into the open the
strange way we perceive the world,
and how that can be changed by film.

STUDENT

Whoo, that is pretty heavy stuff! So he
is saying that the way our mind
perceives can be altered by new modes
of culture and technology. We change
our historical vision?

PROFESSOR

One is tempted to say
"Beam me up Scottie".

STUDENT

I get the feeling that Benjamin is
a bit of a left-field player, coming
from somewhere a bit different?

PROFESSOR

He really does stir things up. Nothing
you are used to is safe from his
very critical analysis. He makes us

83

PROFESSOR (CONT'D)
think a lot about how film and culture
change, and change us. This is a
pretty unsettling idea, but points
to the fact that film (moving image)
really is a radical form of culture.

So Walter Benjamin makes it clear that, for him, in this new age of mechanical reproduction the basic way of looking at a screen and the nature of the film itself has changed so much that the individual no longer contemplates the film per se; the film contemplates them.

He argues that a constantly moving image projected in this mode is a disjunction of the physical process of watching a moving image, and that this changes the structure of perception itself. This is a very radical claim that is much disputed – how this happens and what it means for cultural analysis is not clear.

His question is about how we think of subjectivity in the age of mechanical reproduction. He asks:

BENJAMIN
What does it mean to reflect back onto ourselves our perception of culture after being absorbed by these inauthentic and politicized images?

STUDENT
This just gets more and more complicated. Why do we need to think about it?

PROFESSOR
I guess because we have to try and think about how 'subjectivity' - what it means to be a subject/person - is culturally changed by the nature of film (and TV). This is a seriously difficult question for film theory.

STUDENT
So you mean, what is the cultural impact of film?

PROFESSOR
Precisely, in the sense that it alters the nature of perception, of self-perception, and of the sense of how we live in culture.

PROFESSOR
Actually yes, something like
that. Possibly human nature
changes as the digital world
changes our self-perception.

Because it is such an important essay within film and media studies we will do a quick summary of the main points of Benjamin's major contribution **The Work of Art in the Age of Mechanical Reproduction** (which everyone needs to know):

1. The nature of technological advance transforms the production and consumption of works of art, and of the modes of experiencing those works of art. (This can be called the cultural/technical thesis.)

2. The means of technical reproduction transforms (destroys) the aura of the work of art, undermining its authority through reproduction and liberating the work from history. (Democratization.)

3. New means of technical reproduction, like photography and cinematography, can bring out aspects of the original that escape the naked eye, thus exposing to the viewer the inner life of the work. (The acute radicalism of film.)

4. These new means of reproduction reduce the distance between the object and its viewer, as they can bring the copy into situations which were previously inaccessible for historical and cultural reasons. (Again, a form of democratization of culture.)

5. These changed conditions undermine the unique existence of the original work of art and call into question its authenticity. This allows for the possibility of new forms of art.

key points!

TECHNOLOGICAL ADVANCE

CONSUMPTION

PRODUCTION

6. This change in the status of the work of art holds democratic potential in its ending of the historical elitism of art practices and in technological liberation of the viewer. (The democracy thesis.)

7. In penetrating the illusion of the 'aura' of the work of art, Benjamin draws attention to the historical basis of this notion, to the mystique of authenticity surrounding the original work of art and to its basis in shared sociological experience.

8. The sacred, ritualistic dimension of the work of art is undermined by the processes of cultural/technological transformation and replaced with a new mode of perceiving; of exhibiting rather than of cult status. Film is an important part of this process.

9. Film in particular produces not the individual viewer but the collective subject who approach the work not in a spirit of adulation, but of critique and of disinterestedness. This is the "shock effect" of film.

10. The new kind of viewer is 'distracted' by film, rather than concentrating in the traditional manner, and that distraction is positive in that it confronts the viewer with the contradictions between the work and its reception.

Ultimately Benjamin is arguing that these new forms of cultural technology 'free up' the cultural domain and make culture more accessible and more democratic.

Film theory has often thought about the ways in which its ability to communicate has a strong egalitarian emphasis.

Here's an interesting movie about the guy to follow this up.

http://www.whokilledwalterbenjamin.com/

So already we can see that there are many different ways of thinking about film, and that historical periods and cultures produce different kinds of visions of what film does. However, the question is still:

## What makes a great film, rather than an entertaining film?

There are several different philosophical ways of thinking about film, and although they are clearly inter-related, they can be discussed independently. The main themes are cinema as an institution (how does it all work?), the technologies of filmmaking (how does the development of technology affect film?), the way that film communicates meaning (language and signification) and the textual analysis of films (narrative and story) – along with how ideas are communicated and how people (the audience) receive and understand film. The more you look at film the more you realize what a complicated art-form it is, and because it is so significant in contemporary culture the more important it is to understand it.

STUDENT
I get the feeling that film theory is not anywhere near as straightforward as some people pretend.

PROFESSOR
I have to confess that film and film theory can sometimes be like the guy in the movie-theatre who starts to...

PROFESSOR (CONT'D)

... think that the people in the movie
are real, and shouts at them. Film is
a moving projected image that is a
complete illusion, but it looks real,
and has real consequences, so we have
to think about all of the very odd
steps in that process, from camera, to
image, to projection and the impact on
the human mind and human reaction. It
is no wonder that film theory really is
complex.


STUDENT

I wish I hadn't asked. Can we go
back to basic definitions please?


PROFESSOR

Like 'all film is an illusion
that can pretend to be more real
than the real' or that 'all film
is really like a dream'?


STUDENT

Stop right there.

89

# Chapter 9 André Bazin

The French like to think they invented film, so it is fitting that one of the most important post-war film theorists should be French, and be a philosopher. His basic line was that film could, and should, simply record objective reality, without all this formalist fuss from the Montagists and Expressionists.

André Bazin (1918-1958) wrote a series of essays in the famous *Cahiers du Cinema* journal, which he edited, between the years 1944 and 1958, when he died at the young age of 40. The majority of his essays were translated by Hugh Gray and published in two English volumes: *What is Cinema?* Like all good film theorists Bazin set out to summarise everything about film and its development, and to specify exactly what Realism was, and how it developed. The tendency in film theory to try and dictate precisely what film 'should be' and how it works best is in itself an odd facet of film theory, a prescriptive position which annoys some filmmakers.

his basic line: record objective reality

Bazin, for all his philosophical sophistication as a theorist, has been generally seen as a naïve realist, someone for whom the essence of cinema lay in its mechanical/photographic ability to bring the truth to the screen with minimal human intervention. This is similar to the views of Kracauer, who we discussed earlier.

# Bazin held that the image from a film was an objective re-presentation of the past, a veritable slice of reality.

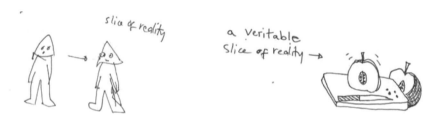

This basic question about how film represents reality keeps coming up in lots of different ways, and is an endlessly fascinating question for film theory, so Bazin spent a lot of time defending his position. What is vital to Bazin's film theory is his philosophical conception of reality, which is based in the phenomenological notion of reality.

Bazin would be obliged to say that the real exists only as perceived, that situations can be said to exist only when a consciousness is engaged with something other than itself. In this view reality is not a completed sphere the mind encounters, but an "emerging-something, which the mind essentially participates in."

For Bazin this is what film does - it creates a new real.

Realism:

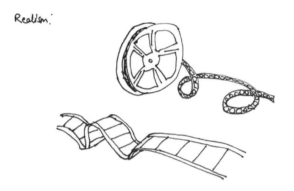

In an important article called *The Evolution of the Language of Film* Bazin argued that Realism was "formally coming of age". By this he meant that the way film represented reality had developed from the pioneers through different types of filmmaking to the high point of 'objective reality', in approaches like Italian Neoealism. Basically for Bazin the cinema is inherently realistic because of the mechanical mediation of the camera. It faithfully reproduces things (which is what people mean by 'naïve Realism'). In an era when film can be created on a computer and looks more real than the real, this approach really does seem outdated.

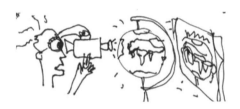

His approach placed him in direct opposition to the radical film theories of the 1920s and 1930s, like Eisenstein and the Expressionists who emphasized how the cinema could manipulate reality. His concentration on objective reality, on using deep focus, and on avoiding montage are linked to his idea that the interpretation of a film or scene should be left to the spectator. Bazin always preferred long takes (which showed 'reality') rather than montage editing. He believed that less was more, and also that narrative was the key to great film. So he liked simple, neorealist films like *The Bicycle Thief.*

Basically Bazin was a bit of a Humanist, and thought all cinema should be idealistic. He said:

> BAZIN
> The cinema substitutes for our gaze a world more in harmony with our desires.

# - as though cinema would make the world a better place?

Here is schematic version of Bazin's idea of how film supposedly developed up to the period when he was writing. He sees it as a struggle towards Realism. So Bazin tries to set out a complete historical model of how cinema develops:

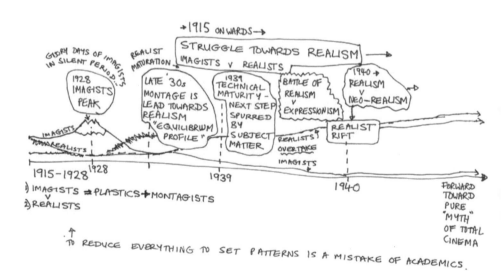

- First we have the Imagists: silent film, anti-Realism, manipulation.

- The Imagists develop the Plastics of film (lighting, decor, composition, acting).

- Then come the Montagists - Eisentein et al. - who develop editing.

- Then the Realists, who develop the long take, on-location shooting and the objective approach.

- According to Bazin, by 1928 the Imagists peak with 1) Expressionism and 2) Soviet Cinema.

- He says that early sound films do not show any advancement of either style.

- By the late '30s, sound techniques force montage toward Realism.

- In the late 30s we also see the perfect fusion of form and content, sound and image.

- Bazin says that film reaches its "equilibrium-profile" (*Jezebel, Stagecoach, Le Jour se Lève*).

- By 1939 all the major technical innovations are completed, and so the next step in the development of style is produced by subject matter.

- Then the big battle. Realism v Expressionism. (The Heavyweights).

- Realism wins in 1940, but the Realists then split into two camps - Real Realism v Neorealism:

  a) Pure objective Realism (Neorealism, documentary, the new reality of film).

  b) Spatial Realism (Jean Renoir, Orson Welles, William Wyler).

This entire schema is really quite odd and demonstrates the academic desire to reduce everything to historical laws. (Filmic reality is much messier and complex.) All sorts of films were made by all sorts of people using many different techniques - and to reduce everything to set patterns is a classic mistake of academics.

The claim of historical progress toward Realism is in perfect accordance with Bazin's theory of the cinema continually moving forward toward the pure 'myth' of total cinema. The line in Bazin's historical evolution theory is that by the 1940s the Imagist style had been completely superceded by the realist style. The Imagists, having had their glory days in the silent period, were confronted by the Realists and, after a realist maturation period in the 30s, were overtaken by them.

Another of Bazin's slightly odd approaches was to argue that cinema was 'an idealistic phenomenon' and only consequently technical, or that the ideas were more important than the technology, whereas clearly technology was important in how film could develop. We can say that Bazin's philosophical desires overrode his historical sense. His basic argument that the function of film was aesthetic was abandoned in the 1960s, when a political revolution in film, and film theory, erupted.

However one thing he did get right was about the Western, when he said:

> BAZIN
> The Western is the only genre whose
> origins are almost identical with
> those of the cinema itself.

> STUDENT
> And you can't get more
> unrealistic than a Western! Even
> if it has nice backdrops.

Remember that Bazin begins and ends with the contention that the best cinema mechanically reproduces reality – so that you sort of have to wish that someone had filmed real cowboys and Indians fighting real battles! Given the fact that most of the Wild West stuff was made up in retrospect, and was mythological, you can see the problem with the idea of Realism in film.

Bazin would have had theoretical kittens if he could ever have seen *Blazing Saddles*.

# Chapter 10 Classic Hollywood and the studio system

## D. W. Griffith (1875-1948) - an `American' beginning.

Film history and film theory are different, but one needs to know some of the history - so let's to go back a bit to look at the amazing (and awful) D. W. Griffith. We can call this section the 'intolerant interlude', because Griffith, a major American filmmaker, was not really a film theorist, and was most definitely a racist, but he changed the nature of filmmaking totally, so we need to talk about him a little bit. Basically he kind of invented the 'blockbuster' movie and, in his dreadful but important film *The Birth of a Nation* (1914),

created the whole thing of a big story, big sets and great big sweeping ideas and emotions. It is based on a play about the Klu Klux Klan and seeks to show how white people are great and how slavery was kind of necessary, because black people are dangerous. So he sort of invented the movies - and also contemporary racism. Pretty weird really. However, as someone said:

```
         MACK SENNETT
D.W. Griffith, when you come right
down to it, invented motion pictures.
As Lionel Barrymore says, there
ought to be a statue to him at
Hollywood and Vine, and it ought
to be fifty feet high, solid gold,
and floodlighted every night.
```

Other people argue that the racism of the film is so abominable that it should be banned, and in fact it is hardly ever watched now. So why is it important, and why do some people describe it as a masterpiece? Well, because it invents and uses all of the tricks of filming and editing that define the possibilities of filmmaking and big movie storytelling, before the Europeans even thought about it. So we can say that the form of the film is radical and impressive but the content (the ideas) are barbaric; another problem for film theory. We can also say that if the first half of *The Birth of a Nation* is a brilliant, absorbing epic that earns its 'masterpiece' label, the second half is a travesty. It is an outpouring of racism, reaction and ignorance that is completely unforgivable.

It seems that the studio also had doubts about their finished product, because the second part of the film opens with the disclaimer: "This is an historical presentation of the Civil War and Reconstruction Period, and is not meant to reflect on any race or people of today."

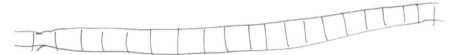

So here we have a great film theory conundrum: does radical 'style' or innovation necessarily produce better films, or is 'style' less important than the ideas and content? Griffith showed what imaginative editing could really do in a film - and the world never looked back. All of these questions come back to haunt us when we look at the Hollywood Classic film. "Coming next", as they say.


## Back to America

In America the institution of film production became highly organized as an industrial studio process that knocked out 'blockbusters', made lots of money, and produced 'stars' who became global figures.

# Hollywood films define what movies are, from *Casablanca* to *Titanic*.

America was always pretty important in the development of film, from silent film, via D.W Griffith, Chaplin and then the studio system through to the world dominance of Hollywood. The giant studios that grew up in Hollywood came to be known as the 'dream factory'- a neat way of describing the industrial scale manufacture of popular entertainment for the masses that produced stars, films and tons of money. It produced what we now describe as 'Classic Hollywood movies'.

Hollywood really was about film as entertainment, or industry, and that is why theorists look at it as a systematic, organized form of capitalist-driven culture. Basically it is argued that film has to be understood not as a simple media text, but as the product of a large cultural organization.

```
            KYRA SEDGWICK
    Hollywood movies are run on fear and
    they don't want to make bold choices.
    They, generally, speaking want to keep
    things status quo. That's not really
    interesting for me.
```

Many people see the start of the Golden Age, which is also known as the 'studio era', as being the year 1927, when **The Jazz Singer**, the first motion picture to have synchronized sound was released. (Actually only bits of it had sound - and in retrospect maybe it shouldn't have.)

the GOLDEN AGE

The Jazz Singer

Classical Hollywood is a theoretical term used to describe the period of time beginning in the late1920s through the late 1950s (some people give earlier and later dates). Many have called this period the Golden Age of Hollywood movies. You could call all the studio films during this period 'classic film products'.

100

Of course somebody had to develop a theory about it, so we have Classic Hollywood film theory, which is another attempt to classify and describe a whole set of films within a given paradigm. It is in theoretical terms about what we might call a mode of production: a particular style, editing technique and visual means of constructing a film.

One German director sums up a rather interesting conundrum about film and Hollywood:

ROLAND EMMERICH
It's like everybody is obsessed with Hollywood movies worldwide. And even though everybody hates the Americans, they're still watching American movies.

# So what is Classic Hollywood cinema?

Basically it is a term that was dreamed up by David Bordwell, Janet Staiger and Kristin Thompson in their important book of the same name, *Classical Hollywood Cinema*. In this study the authors performed a formalist analysis of a random selection of 100 Hollywood films from 1917 to 1960. That is to say that they looked at the formal construction and elements of particular films, at how they were put together and how they worked. They then came to the conclusion that during this period a distinctive cinematic style developed that could be called Classical Hollywood style. The authors then go on to claim that this style has become universal (or paradigmatic) because of the global dominance of Hollywood cinema.

STUDENT
What about alternative films?

PROFESSOR
They exist, but Hollywood really does dominate mainstream cinema is basically American, in loads of countries. The most political claim that the authors have made is that filmmakers anywhere face a choice between two stark alternatives. Either they succumb to the Classical Hollywood style and follow its narrative example, or they try and revolt against it and attempt to deliberately undermine or subvert that style (alternative films).

## STEVEN SPIELBERG

I wanted to do another movie that
could make us laugh and cry and feel
good about the world. I wanted to
do something else that could make
us smile. This is a time when we
need to smile more and Hollywood
movies are supposed to do that
for people in difficult times.

STUDENT
So what are the most important elements
of the classical Hollywood style?

PROFESSOR
We might say a story, with a
beginning, a middle and an end.
Another key element of the classical
style is built on the key principle of
continuity editing or 'invisible'
style. This is where as smooth
naturalism is dominant and this is
created as a style in which the camera
and the sound recording never call
attention to themselves, and the
'invisible' editing creates the
illusion of a seamless story. The
viewer doesn't have to do any work in
terms of understanding the film.

Continuity editing...

'Invisible style'

a Seamless story

Here are some top Hollywood movies, as agreed by experts – in no
particular order:

- *Sunset Boulevard (1950)*

- *Gone With The Wind (1939)*

- *All About Eve (1950)*

- *White Heat (1949)*
- *Mr Skeffington (1944)*
- *Wizard Of Oz (1939)*
- *Jezebel (1938)*
- *Yankee Doodle Dandy (1942)*
- *Of Human Bondage (1934)*
- *That Hamilton Woman (1941)*
- *The Man Who Knew Too Much (1956)*
- *Wuthering Heights (1939)*
- *To Have And Have Not (1944)*
- *Love Me Or Leave Me (1955)*
- *The Big Sleep (1946)*
- *Grand Hotel (1932)*
- *Key Largo (1948)*
- *The Life Of Emile Zola (1937)*
- *Casablanca (1942)*
- *Vertigo (1958)*
- *Humoresque (1946)*
- *Double Indemnity (1944)*
- *Dinner At Eight (1933)*
- *Titanic (1953)*
- *From Here To Eternity (1953)*
- *Treasure Of Sierra Madre (1948)*
- *High Noon (1952)*
- *Some Like It Hot (1959)*
- *Notorious (1946)*
- *A Star Is Born (1954)*
- *Vertigo (1958)*
- *Singin' In The Rain (1952)*

Bordwell, Staiger and Thompson have given an extensive answer to the question of defining a Hollywood Classic movie and it is quite a complicated debate which readers can take up. Here we provide an explanation which just looks at the basics :

## 1.  Narrative (the story)

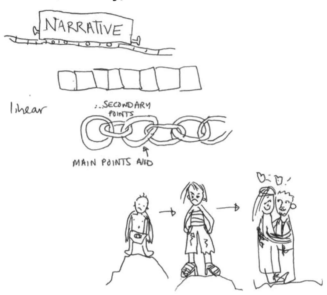

This is about how the story is told, and the way in which it is told. As in classical novels there are main protagonists, and events that are linear (follow each other), and which can be easily grasped through obvious patterns of cause and effect. The narrative is clearly organized with a clear beginning, middle and end. The story almost always has a clear resolution (a happy ending). The characters' aims are usually psychological (individual) rather than social or political. The plot is character-driven and heroes are commonplace.

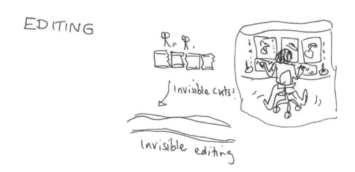

## 2. **Editing**

The way the film is cut together. (Somebody sits in a room somewhere and spends many, many hours editing all of the film that has been shot.)

Perhaps the single most important element of cinematic form, or organization, that characterizes classical Hollywood cinema is that of continuity editing (sometimes called 'invisible editing'). The aim of this continuity editing is to make the cut invisible, so that the whole film looks naturalistic (or real). The editing is subsidiary to the flow of the narrative and the editing is done in a way that does not draw attention to itself (whereas alternative films often use editing to draw attention to the nature of film). This is Hollywood illusion.

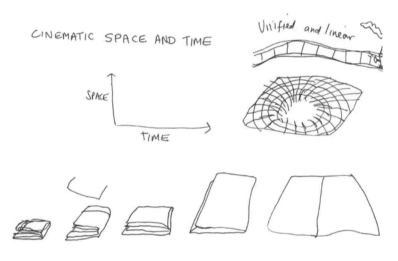

In terms of film theory itself we need to think about the way that cinematic space and time are used (the way that objects and movement are presented in the film) in Hollywood

## 3. **Producing Realism (naturalism)**

We say that both space and time are 'constructed' in cinema, by which we mean that the idea of space and time is represented in a particular way in any give film. In the classical Hollywood movie space and time are presented as continuous and linear - reality which appears seamless. One thing happens after another, presented as a unified whole to match our ordinary everyday perception of time and space. So it appears as though you are there watching events unfold, just like in normal life.

107

<pre>
                    ET
    I've got an idea for a movie - if
    you've got the time I've got the
    space.
</pre>

## 4. **Three-act narrative**

A classic idea that goes back to Aristotle, but which has been investigated in the twentieth century by people who look at the structure of narrative (the Formalists). The plots are structured around orientation, complication and resolution. The story sets out, something happens to mess things up and then everything gets resolved. (As in the 'boy gets girl' movie – the most basic plot line of all.) Resolution is what makes people happy; things on the screen get fixed, unlike in real life!

## 5. **Objective storytelling**

Everything is made clear so the viewer knows more than the characters do, and everything is understood, so the audience has a seemingly 'objective' view of what is going on. Once again it is about representing the world as obvious and straightforward, which often leads to stereotypes - like the 'tart with a golden heart'. Cynics might say that the films are dumbed down for the mass market, but we couldn't comment on this.

ORIENTATION

COMPLICATION

RESOLUTION

Classic Hollywood movies can be described as 'organized illusion' that tells a good story and always ends with a clearly understood resolution (producing happiness and reassurance – most of the time).

GIRL
Hey Mum, why does Superman always win?

The question for film theory is:

# Is this therefore a reactionary form of entertainment that reinforces the dominant ideology?

# A quick summary by Bordwell:

**BORDWELL**
We can argue that the unifying force
behind the classical Hollywood style
is motivation and conventions. In the
development of the narrative every
event is motivated, i.e. follows a
causal relationship. In the same
way the use of cinematic style is
generally motivated by the narrative.
The connection between narrative and
cinematic style is highly conventional.

**STUDENT**
In other words Classic Hollywood
narrative is the bog-standard way of
making an easy-to-watch film that has
a good story, everyone can understand
it, and the good guy always wins.

**PROFESSOR**
That really is pretty much how it
works. The question is has this
Bordwell fellow come up with a
theory that encompasses all of
the movies, all of the time?

**STUDENT**
Is the theory too general maybe,
given that there are so many
different kinds of films?

**PROFESSOR**
As the man said, "Here's
looking at you kid."

**STUDENT**
... and why do they call Hollywood
the 'dream factory'? Actually I
know the answer to that question.

# Industry and organization

In terms of film theory we can see that the sociological question of power, money and influence is quite a big one. Hollywood is indeed a very powerful institution in terms of output, influence and cultural dominance (sometimes called cultural imperialism by those who don't like it).

We might say that Europe seems to have a love/hate relationship with Hollywood.

**Some key questions:**

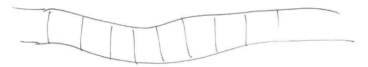

- Is the socio-economic organization of the film industry a key determinant of its output?

- Does the drive for entertainment lead to the production of ideologically conformist narrative (mass entertainment).

- Is film a form of escapism that contributes to political conformity (popular culture)?

- Have multi-media conglomerates in today's world re-captured control of most film production?

- Most importantly, is it possible to make critical films within the dominant industry framework?

- Is the distribution of movies another absolutely key factor in controlling the industry?

- Should one go to the Cannes film festival?

# ... and now for something completely different.

# Chapter 11 Italian Neorealism

A good deal of film theory developed in reaction to the Hollywood model, since it was, and pretty much still is, the dominant model. Any kind of radical filmmaking tried to distance itself from Hollywood's influence, and Italian Neorealism was explicitly trying to do this.

Neorealism was a quite short-lived but hugely influential film movement that was based in a specific idea of how films should be made. A reasonable summary of what the movement was about is to say that in the period after the 2nd World War the Neorealists developed a specific mode of cinema to describe and capture the terrible hardships of everyday life in a country devastated by the war. It was a response to a social crisis, and to a changing world.

IT WAS A RESPONSE

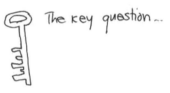

The key question ...

The key question was how to represent social reality in all its grittiness and harsh truth. It was a reaction to Hollywood, to escapism and to the glossy propaganda films, which were called 'white telephone' movies, that had been knocked out by the Fascist regime of Mussolini. It was a film movement that wanted to show the world as it was, to be a people's cinema, and to adopt a mode of filmmaking that was truthful and 'realistic' but also lyrical and moral. It was quite revolutionary in its transformation of film.

White
telephone
movies

MAN ON WHITE PHONE
Can you send someone up to
polish my morals for me...

STUDENT
So what were the neorealist films like?

PROFESSOR
They were lyrical, critical,
**understated, sometimes crude** films that
tried to create a sense of everyday
reality, and its complexities and
beauties, through a blend of 'real'
actors, and 'real' life, as though
reality could be reinterpreted
through the camera. (as opposed to
the smoothness of Hollywood).

PROFESSOR
One screenwriter(Guiseppe de Santis)
described the films as being very
proletarian and steeped "in the air of
death and sperm" - whatever that means.
This was about making films that
showed 'real-life', warts and all,
and examined what made society, and
history, tick. Neorealism started life,
then, as a political and aesthetic
movement, not as a theoretical idea
or a set of theories. It was about
creating a 'sense of reality'.

Roberto Rossellini's 1945 film **Roma, Città Aperta (Open City)** is probably the preeminent example of this approach to filmmaking, along with Vittoria de Sica's **The Bicycle Thief** (1948) and **Fellini's La Strada** (1954), and there are many others.

Martin Scorcese described Italian Neorealism as "the most precious moment in film history." He probably meant by this that the kind of cinematic beauty and truth that Neorealism produced has disproportionally influenced many filmmakers since the 1950s, particularly the Nouvelle Vague in France - and almost everybody concerned with politically motivated art. The cinema of the developing countries has also been influenced strongly by this style and approach.

Scorcese

Neorealism consisted mainly of the canonical trio of Roberto Rossellini, Vittoria De Sica and Visconti, plus sometimes Pasolini. What they were doing is precisely summed up in this quote:

```
                PASOLINI
      Right after the war, passions were so
      strong that they really pushed us,
      they forced towards this kind of film
      truth. And this truth was transfigured
      by poetry, and lyricism. It was because
```

PASOLINI (CONT'D)
... of its lyricism that Neorealism
so captured the world. Because
there was poetry in our reality.


So, although political, Neorealism was also an aesthetic movement.
Federico Fellini, in a interesting interview from 1961, reinforces the
importance of aesthetics, saying that:


FELLINI
Neorealism is not about what you show,
but how you show it. It's simply a way
of looking at the world without
preconceptions or prejudices. Some
people are still convinced that
Neorealism should only be used to show
a particular type of reality - social
reality to be exact. But then it
becomes propaganda.

The lyricism of the filmmaking, the use of real locations and often
also non-actors, gives the films a power and intensity not found
in traditional narrative films. Roberto Rossellini, one of Italian
Neorealism's key directors, defined this approach as:


ROSSELLINI
... above all a moral position from
which to look at the world.

Rossellini

# Influences of Neorealism

Anti-Hollywood sentiment goes quite a long way in film theory and this was to prove the case with Italian Neorealism. **Rome Open City** is one of the great landmarks of cinema because of the way it changed everyone's thinking, and because of the way it was made just as Rome was liberated from the Nazis. The sense of urgency and political importance were new, and changed what film could do - forever.

The first Neorealist picture, which was probably **Ossessione (1943)** by Visconti, was made more than 70 years ago, but the movement still fascinates everyone. It influenced the British New Wave and the French Nouvelle Vague. Many Italian directors are still grappling with it, from the Taviani brothers **(Caesar Must Die, 2012)** to the younger generation such as Matteo Garrone **(Gomorrah, 2008; Reality, 2012)**.

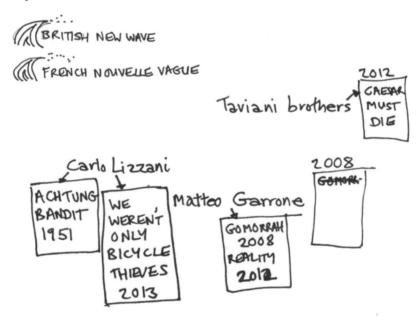

BRITISH NEW WAVE

FRENCH NOUVELLE VAGUE

2012
CAESAR MUST DIE

Taviani brothers

Carlo Lizzani

2008
GOMORR-

ACHTUNG BANDIT 1951

WE WEREN'T ONLY BICYCLE THIEVES 2013

Matteo Garrone

GOMORRAH 2008
REALITY 2012

Later, in 2013, one of the last surviving Neorealists, 91-year-old Carlo Lizzani (**Achtung Bandit! 1951, The Verona Trial 1962)** released a documentary entitled **We Weren't Only Bicycle Thieves**, which includes contributions from Bernardo Bertolucci, Paolo and Vittorio Taviani, Martin Scorsese, Steven Spielberg, Ridley Scott, Ron Howard - and many others.

In Britain, Neorealism influenced the 1960s' revolt against the very British kinds of realist war films and costume dramas that were the main stay of the industry.

Cesare Zavattini, who functions as a kind of godfather of the movement, stated:

```
              ZAVATTINI
This powerful desire of the
[Neorealist] cinema to see and to
analyze, this hunger for reality, for
truth, is a kind of concrete homage to
other people, that is, to all who
exist.
```

Cesare
Zavattini

Neorealism's aim, method and philosophy was fundamentally
Humanist: to show Italian life without embellishment and without
artifice. Breezy fare this is not, but it did significantly alter European
filmmaking and eventually cinema around the world.

As director Giuseppe Bertolucci (Bernardo's brother) noted:

                    BERTOLUCCI
        The cinema was born with Neorealism.

Giuseppe Bertolucci

                BERTOLUCCI (CONT'D)
        Not Rossellini though. Rossellini
        is the only one in Neorealism who
        didn't just show us things, didn't
        just try to be a realist, but gave
        us an idea of things. He wasn't
        interested in the appearance of
        things, but in the idea behind the
        things. Even the idea behind the idea.

It was this definition by Brecht that critically challenged Italian
Neorealism:

                    BRECHT
        Realism doesn't mean showing
        real things, but showing
        how things really are.

                    STUDENT
        So where are we now with film theory?

PROFESSOR

Well, I think we can say that after
the 2nd World War the role of film
changed a lot. Film tried to deal
with the realities of the war, but
it was also heavily implicated in
propaganda and, after the war, in
rebuilding images of national cultures
and identities. So probably film theory
lagged behind all the political and
social changes that were going on.
Bazin tried to create a total theory
of film which, perhaps for a while,
seemed dominant, but difficult questions
of people, power and politics in the
end overwhelmed his neat theorizing.


STUDENT

And why was Italian Neorealism
so influential?


PROFESSOR

I think because it fused the questions
of form, genre and politics into
a coherent, almost poetic style
which allowed a deeper sense of
social reality to emerge in film.
Hollywood just kept on churning out
the polished entertainment it was
so good at, but in the rest of the
world film was developing all sorts of
different roles, and it wasn't until
later that film theory started to
catch up with all of these changes.


STUDENT

So what were the new questions
for film theory?


PROFESSOR

Well there was the question of the
role of film after Auschwitz, meaning
how did film as an art form deal with
the horrors of the 2nd World War. Then
there was the question of politics
and power: how did film deal with the
realities of politics, oppression
and Imperialism, questions that were
being raised all over the globe?

PROFESSOR (CONT'D)
To put it succinctly we can say
that questions of ideology and
power, and film's relationship to
them, were now becoming central.


STUDENT
And I thought it was getting easier?!

We can say that the Expressionism and Montagism of the 1930s were overturned as the dominant film theory in the post 2nd World War era by both Neorealism and André Bazin's new approach. When the 1960s kicked in, by which we mean the political upheavals that spread across America and Europe, all the old certainties in film theory were kicked into touch. At the same time there were things going on in film in some of the Eastern European communist countries, and in developing countries. Film theory was just coming of age, and growing up as a discipline - and now it went in all directions, heavily influenced by new strands of thought from psychoanalysis, Structuralism, semiotics, Feminism and Marxist theories of anti-capitalist propaganda. (Film theory as a discipline really started in the 1960s.)

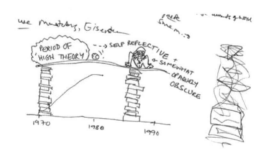

The Hollywood machine mostly just kept on pumping out 'entertainment', steadfastly ignoring experimentation, radicalism, revolution and any non-genre style that might interfere with the money-making, easy-to-watch, populist and sentimentalist movies. However there was, even in Hollywood, sometimes a sense of the darker side of things - and it was out of this that Film Noir developed.

So what is Film Noir

Orson Welles

Fritz Lang

Billy Wilder

# Chapter 12 Film Noir

Funnily enough it was some French critics who seem to have coined the term 'Film Noir' but this movement (or style) actually emerged in America. Some people even argue that Film Noir is one of Hollywood's only organic artistic movements. *The Big Sleep* (1946) and *The Big Heat* (1953) are taken to be two of the key films in this genre.

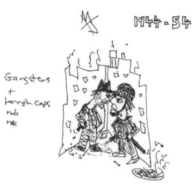

So what is Film Noir? Well, it usually has an urban, often detective-based story, set in a grimy, down-town, dark environment where gangsters and tough cops rub noses. Film Noir really derived from the tough-guy detective fiction of Dashiell Hammett and Raymond Chandler, and presented a world that was quite different from the sentimental family based melodrama of standard Hollywood fare. The dangerous, the repressed and the menacing are elements that came from German Expressionism.

PROFESSOR
Film Noir is a style or genre of cinematographic film, marked by a mood of pessimism, fatalism, and menace. The term was originally applied (by a group of French critics) to American thriller or detective films made in the period 1944-54 and to the work of directors such as Orson Welles, Fritz Lang, and Billy Wilder.

Interestingly many of these movies were made by European émigré directors who shared a certain European storytelling sensibility, which was highly stylized, quite theatrical, and with imagery often drawn from an earlier era of German expressionist cinema. These 'black films' or rather dark American thrillers had a touch of Neorealism about them. Their production was largely fuelled by the financial and artistic success of Billy Wilder's classic adaptation of James M. Cain's novella **Double Indemnity** (1944). After this the studios began churning out crime thrillers and murder dramas which had a particularly dark and cynical view of existence.

To this day the debate goes on as to whether 'Noir' is a proper film genre, delineated by its content, or simply a style of storytelling, identified by its visual style (Noirism?)

In a way Film Noir negates the Classic Hollywood thesis since it was Hollywood knocking out these slightly radical films!

JOHN BRILEY
[Film Noir] experiences periodic
rebirth and rediscovery. Whenever we
have any moment of deep societal rift
or disruption in America, one of the
ways we can express it is through the
ideas and behavior in Film Noir.

# Chapter 13 Auteur theory

Auteur theory | LATE 1940's ⟶ Film-maker as author, or *auteur*

Sometime in the late 1940s, some French critics, including André Bazin and Alexandra Astruc, came up with a new theory, which insisted on the importance of the filmmaker as author, or auteur. This was taken up by the film theorists around the **Cahiers du Cinema** journal and became quite influential. At first glance it is a pretty simple theory: that a film director can be seen as the individual 'author' of the film, just as a painter controls the finished painting.

DIRECTOR

This auteur theory, which was actually derived from Astruc's development of the concept of caméra-stylo ('camera-pen'), really says that it is as though the director draws the picture by overseeing all the audio and visual elements of the motion picture; bringing them all together. So the director - rather than the writer or producer, or the team - is the 'author' of the movie.

Astruc's elaboration of the concept caméra-stylo ("camera-pen")

Director draws the picture

overseeing Audio Visual

There are strong and weak points about this theory which we will come to later. As Andrew Sarris, the film critic who championed the theory, said:

ANDREW SARRIS
The strong director imposes his own personality on a film; the weak director allows the personalities of others to run rampant.

*So to be thought of as an 'auteur'*

So, to be thought of as an 'auteur' you need to have a strong and individual style that can be seen in all your films. Somebody like Hitchcock is a clear candidate. You can spot one of his films from behind a shower curtain.

Jean-Luc Godard and François Truffaut, two important French filmmakers, took up this theory - possibly because they wanted to be seen as 'auteurs' rather than just as run-of-the-mill directors. They are seen as New Wave critics and it was in fact Truffaut who first

*New wave critics*

coined the phrase "la politique des auteurs" in his article *Une Certaine Tendance du Cinéma Français*. He basically argued that the best directors (like him) have a distinctive style, which can be recognized through consistent themes and aesthetic ideas running throughout their films. This new wave idea says that it is this individual creative vision that makes the director the true author of the film. So an auteur must have a differentiating style, which is almost instantly recognisable.

*consistent themes and aesthetic ideas running through films*

Truffaut championed Hitchcock as being an auteur for exactly these reasons, and then himself. Any good theory should lead to self-improvement!

> TRUFFAUT
> The film of tomorrow will resemble the
> person who made it, and the number of
> spectators will be proportional to the
> number of friends the director has.

So we could ask 'what use is auteur theory'? Well, it clearly identifies a way of thinking about the manner in which a director imposes his artistic vision on the film, through the use of styles, techniques and patterns in order to create a particular artistic vision. This is fine for filmmakers who set out to make very stylistically distinctive films, and are individualistic in their outlook, but it rather skates over the questions about cinematography, editing, sound, script and all the other things that go into a film. Perhaps this individualistic idea was something to do with the rejection of authoritarian systems that occurred after the Second World War. It was also the case that American films were banned under the German occupation, so when they returned there was a powerful intensity to watching them.

As the man said:

> TRUFFAUT
> What switched me to films was the
> flood of American pictures into
> Paris after the Liberation.

The French have always had a thing about film and Truffaut and everyone wanted to be a filmmaker. Back then you either had to serve a long apprenticeship as an assistant director or get government funding on short film courses. The New Wave were going to do it their way.

The Cahiers group, being young and impatient, rejected both of these approaches. This was what being the New Wave meant, you had to re-invent everything. They decided they would have to bypass the rules of the existing system if they wanted to break into the film industry and make the kind of films they thought necessary. So while building up the profile of the *Cahiers du Cinema* magazine, they carefully gained experience and contacts. Claude Chabrol worked as a publicist at 20th Century-Fox, Jean-Luc Godard worked as a press agent. François Truffaut worked as an assistant for Max Ophuls and Roberto Rossellini and Jean Rivette worked with both Jean Renoir and Jacques Becker.

<pre>
                        GODARD
            Photography is truth. The cinema is
            truth twenty-four times per second.
</pre>

This Nouvelle group were very lucky, as the French government itself began to intervene in filmmaking, and made funding and distribution available. French culture was seen as being under attack from Hollywood. Fortunately, at the same time, some interesting technological developments meant that filmmaking equipment was becoming much cheaper. There were new, lightweight, hand-held cameras, which were developed for use in documentary making and there were faster film stocks which required less light, and which could work with more portable sound and lighting equipment. These changes meant filmmakers no longer needed to be in a studio to make a film, which was a major shift. The Cahier boys could now go out with small budgets and shoot on location using smaller crews and real backdrops, such as Paris. Working in this way encouraged experimentation and improvisation and gave the directors more control – which may have led indirectly to the auteur theory.

The French-American relation in film is quite interesting, a sort of love-hate that keeps swinging from one extreme to the other. Oddly, it was an American, Andrew Sarris, who took up and extolled autuer theory and made it an important part of thinking about film.

In Sarris' book *The American Cinema: Directors and Directions 1929-1968* he explained and developed the idea of the auteur. He used it to tell the story of American filmmaking which he did by analyzing the careers and work of a number of individuals, classifying them according to their respective talents and their imprint on their own films.

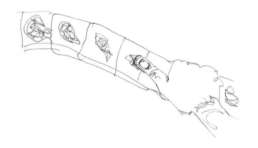

ANDREW SARRIS
Over a group of films a director
must exhibit certain recurrent
characteristics of style, which
serve as his signature.

Sarris' approach then led him to try and form a canon of great
directors (whereas the French critics had never claimed the concept
to be a theory). Like many academics he wanted to 'own' the theory,
which is also often a problem in the world of film theory - but as
somebody said "What about the guys who just make movies?"

STUDENT
So, how would you try and work
out if someone was an 'auteur'?

PROFESSOR
You need to show that the director
uses consistent ideas and elements
throughout all of his work,
that they have an oeuvre.

STUDENT
An egg?

PROFESSOR
No, that means a body of work, so we
say that Ingmar Bergman created a
consistent body of films, an oeuvre,
which share common concerns and ideas.

To summarize, we need to show that an auteur is the absolute master of their filmmaking and that they display all of the relevant required characteristics (like ego-mania).

1. The visual style (mise-en-scène and cinematography) is consistent – and noticeably different. (Bergman)

2. Specific character traits/situations re-occur in the films. (Chaplin)

3. Narrative structures and patterns are consistent/repeated. (Hitchcock)

4. A set of themes is dealt with in the body of films. (Godard)

If we use this approach then really only a few directors come into the auteur category - many directors make quite different sorts of movies over time. Orson Welles is a great director who made one brilliant film, *Citizen Kane,* and many other films - but they were different and quite often bad. And although he could be called the auteur of *Citizen Kane* the other films wouldn't count (moreover, the brilliant script of *Citizen Kane* was written by someone else). This makes the point that films are actually made by a lot of people, and that ultimately it is a collaborative process.

# If you write, direct, act, shoot, design, edit, and score the film, then you have stronger ground to stand on.

Smaller Crews

Just to throw another theoretical spanner into the works – classic auteur theory is out of sync with many current theories about reading/interpretation, as well as current theories of subjectivity or identity or of 'the individual' (in this case, the author or director). Barthes and Foucault in the late 1960s each in their own inimitable way challenged the idea of the author as the originator of the meaning of a work. Barthes's famous essay, **The Death of the Author** maintains that a text has multiple layers and meanings (not all of which are the deliberate construction of the 'author') and that instead of looking at the author for 'the original intended meaning', we should look to the readers/viewers for various possible meanings. Or, to put it another way, films can be interpreted differently by different people.

Also, Foucault's famous essay **What is an Author?** suggests that an author is an intersection of various social and culture discourses (ideas, values, images, ways of thinking, style) which are circulating at any given time – therefore in a sense an author (or auteur) is a mouthpiece rather than a visionary individual or 'creator' of meaning. So a film is unlikely to have a specific author.

At first auteur theory seems like a perfectly good theory: the director is responsible for every aspect of the film and so it should be easy to say whether or not they are an auteur. However, more than one person will work on a film (like, hundreds), so what makes the director more responsible than, say, the script-writer or the actors, or the camera operators? You could argue that the director has the ultimate control, and is therefore responsible for the film's final shape and tone. But in what is a totally collective medium, it is almost impossible to establish who really has the most control. It is a bit like looking at the manager of a football team. Is he responsible for the total performance of the team? ("Oy, you! You're fired! Get me another manager.")

Another problem with auteur theory is that it creates a hierarchy within film criticism. Those who believe in it would automatically assume that an auteur is a better filmmaker than an 'ordinary' director, even though he or she might make really good and important films.

The most common examples given to support auteur theory are Alfred Hitchcock, Stanley Kubrick, Jean-Luc Godard and Tim Burton.

Andrew Sarris, in defending auteur theory, went along with Truffaut's individualism, seeing the author-subject as the origin of creative genius - which was like a red rag to a poststructuralist bull. For Foucault and Barthes the idea of the author-subject was a nonsense; for them there were only determining structures that operated through historical changes. Film was seen by them as a complex product of a complex set of structures that operated like a machine: the 'apparatus', as Metz would later put it. The humanism and individualism of auteur theory were to be thoroughly undermined by later film theory, and the ideas of semiotics and ideological signifying systems replaced any notions of creativity.

Scorsese

Geoffrey Nowell-Smith, a British writer, tried to construct an auteur-structuralism which said that the author was really a set of structural relations that could be found in the work of the filmmakers' - it has a sort of set of identifying features.

                    NOWELL-SMITH
        The purpose of criticism becomes
        therefore to uncover behind the
        superficial contrast of subject and
        treatment a structural hard core of
        basic and often recondite motifs.

This attempt to rescue auteur theory was not given much time of day by the bad boys of the later structuralist movement, who rounded up the individuals and had them shipped off to a reservation. Structures ruled OK.

Two later French theorists who had impacts on film theory were
Deleuze and Guattari. Their complex Structuralism is an example
of the density of potential work, here they are making an effort to
give an adequate accounting of the relationship between word and
image, as it applies to film theory. They say in *A Thousand Plateaus:*

> DELEUZE & GUATTARI
> This is what we call the abstract
> machine, which constitutes and
> conjugates all of the assemblage's
> cutting edges of deterritorialization.

> STUDENT
> This makes it very clear exactly
> what one should think about thinking
> about film! (This is a filmic joke.)

> PROFESSOR
> Too many auteurs spoil the wrath.

> OSBORNE
> There are many roads to making
> a film and none of them lead
> back to where we started.

# Chapter 14 Marxist analysis of film

Jean-Luc Comolli

Jean Narboni

Two more radical French film theorists who also wrote for *Cahiers du Cinema* were Jean-Luc Comolli & Jean Narboni. According to them, and from a Marxist perspective, the debates about auteurism and Realism missed the point. Film was part of the dominant ideological apparatus and that was that. They asserted this dogmatically, and this pretty much sums up their entire approach:

Jean Narboni

COMOLLI & NARBONI
The classic film theory of cinema that the camera is an impartial instrument that grasps, or rather is impregnated by, the world in its 'concrete reality' is an eminently reactionary one. What the camera in fact registers is the vague, un-formulated, un-theorized, un-thought-out world of the dominant ideology. Cinema is one of the languages through which the world communicates itself to itself. They constitute its ideology for they reproduce the world as it is experienced when filtered through its ideology.

Film is therefore basically mostly ideology, reproducing the dominant ideas of the society, a capitalist society, which seeks to keep its citizens in thrall to the idea that their place in society is what it is, and probably always will be. This is much like the idea that Hollywood narrative is a form of escapist entrapment that provides "opium for the masses". As far as they were concerned, film had to confront ideology and had to seek to liberate people from illusions.

Therefore, according to Comolli and Narboni, to stop film from just becoming the "tool" of the dominant world-view:

COMOLLI & NARBONI
The filmmaker's first task is to show up the cinema's so-called 'depiction of reality'.

If the filmmaker is able to achieve that, they might be able to "sever" or "disrupt" the "connection between the cinema and its ideological function". For Comolli and Narboni Realism is simply a reproduction, on the screen, of the repressive ideological structures we encounter in everyday life, the sense that the world cannot change. Therefore the realist aesthetic completely fails to challenge or explore the structures of the dominant ideology and world view in society and art, it is reactionary. So, they argue, film cannot challenge or explore sexist, racist or oppressive ideologies – it is a failed critique and a redundant social activity; art without the ability to challenge or explore social attitudes is not really art at all. Film therefore has to be revolutionary. This is very much the same set of ideas that inform the radical Third Cinema approach.

COMOLLI & NARBONI
As a result of being a material product of the system, film is also an ideological product of the system.

This hard line approach was popular for a while - but there are so many problems with it that it is difficult to know where to start. The idea that films could tell a story or even be entertaining is just seen as delusion - it is a moral stance that is actually puritanal rather than Marxist.

More
Puritan
than
Marxist

Comolli & Narboni produced a list of films that they categorised as bad, not so bad, awful, reactionary, and a few that are ideologically acceptable - they may be dull, but they are worthy.

Overall the Marxist approaches to thinking about film are great for looking at the general sociological understanding of film as an industry, and the role that film can play in propaganda and escapism. Where they kind of collapse is they are really not very useful at talking about how film actually works, how audiences actually react to films, and the many complicated questions about how films 'mean' different things.

Here is a nice example of a film question that Marxism wouldn't be too good at answering: We have **Postman Pat** and **Bob the Builder**, animated cartoons that are much loved around the world. What would a Marxist analysis of **Postman Pat** look like? The question of animated films is a whole other area of film theory that we really haven't touched on, for reasons of space, but it is clear at least that questions about Realism and stuff would get a bit squishy when talking about **Postman Pat**.

There is another dimension to the cultural questions around **Postman Pat** and **Bob the Builder** which is about how audiences from different cultures interpret things. In Japan, for example, the Yakuza gangsters chop off one of their fingers to prove their gangster credentials. **Postman Pat** and **Bob the Builder** both have one digit short of a full hand (check out the animation). So it is quite possible that in Japan they could be read as symbolic of the Yakuza. This was a real worry when the films were exported there. The issue here is about what is called 'encoding' and de-coding', which means how messages are put into films (en-coding) and how they can be read (de-coding) which often will not be the same. Stuart Hall, the British cultural theorist developed these very useful ideas. It is not known what the Yakuza think about **Postman Pat**, or Marxist theories of film, but we do know that there quite a few good Japanese films about gangsters. (Something else there isn't room to talk about here.)

From the film **The Yakuza** (1974):

```
                    DUSTY
        American saw cuts on a push stroke,
        Japanese saw cuts on a pull stroke.
        When an American cracks up, he opens
        up the window and shoots up a bunch
        of strangers. When a Japanese cracks
        up, he closes the window and kills
        himself. Everything is in reverse.
```

# Chapter 15 Genre theory

Another important, and more mainstream, approach to examining film in the most general sense is that of genre theory. (Westerns are an example of the most obvious and typical genre films).

Genre is a sort of upmarket word for a type - Godzilla movies are of a particular type or genre. Novels were historically put into genres - like detective novels, romantic novels, adventure novels and so on. So this is applied to films and they are classified into genres, which is quite a useful way of describing things.

To be technical the word 'genre' comes from the French (originally Latin) word for 'kind' or 'class', so we are talking about a particular 'kind' or 'class' of film.

**COWBOY**
When I walk into a saloon and say
"Howdy, give me a whiskey" I might be
walking into a genre trap.

**BARMAN**
If that is a joke then you need
an Englishman and an Irishman
to go along with it.

Cowboy shoots barman.

STUDENT
Why do we need a genre theory? Can't
we just talk about directors?

PROFESSOR
Well actually if you think about how
films are sold to the public they are
mostly sold by category - as in: this
one is a great comedy film, this one is
a romance, etc. If you didn't have
genres people wouldn't know where they
were.

STUDENT
Yeh, like science fiction movies,
or action thrillers.

PROFESSOR
Precisely. And given that the Hollywood
industry churns them out at a rate of
knots, viewers need some help so they
don't end up watching the wrong film.
If you think about Blockbusters video
rental it was all organized in genres.

141

STUDENT
Does every film belong to a
genre, or just most of them?


PROFESSOR
That is the really tricky question,
and we have to talk about sub-genres.

STUDENT
Is that about films set on submarines?
I liked *The Hunt for Red October.*


PROFESSOR
Well, almost right - it means a sub-
division of a main genre and sub films
probably are a sub-sub genre.

Genre theory comes from literature and probably goes back to the Greek philosophers who liked to put things in categories. In essence this is what genre theory is doing – categorising films into different kinds that we can recognize. In particular, fictional films are categorized according to their setting, characters, themes, topic mood, or format. You need to look at these characteristics to identify a genre.

1. Typical mise-en-scène. The setting is the milieu or the environment in which the story and action unfolds, like Westerns which are set out in the 'rough and ready' West. Gangster films are almost invariably set in grimy cities, and so on.

2. Typical types of narrative. The stories, themes or topic of a genre film refers to the issues or concepts that the film deals with. The recent crop of vampire films is a clear genre, and a bit of a pain in the neck. Road movies are all about travelling, again usually somehow in the West.

3. Typical style/mood. The mood is the overall emotional tone of the film - comedies are meant to be funny, and horror films are meant to be scary.

4. Typical editing style – visual appearance. Most horror movies are quickly recognisable through certain tricks/atmosphere.

5. Typical dialogue, sound track, ways of talking etc. (Spaghetti Westerns)

6. Typical actors, directors, generic types/roles. The bad guy and the good guy in Westerns and super hero movies.

7. The format refers to how the film was made, eg 35mm, 16mm, 8mm or digital, or the manner of presentation., eg widescreen, 3D, cinemascope, or the manner of presentation.

Another way of thinking about film genres is by looking at the target audience. Some film theorists argue that actually neither format nor target audience are in themselves film genres, but we still talk about 'teen' films, or 'action' movies, as though genres do exist. As we said earlier too, film genres often branch out in subgenres, as in the case of the courtroom and trial-focused subgenre of drama, now known as legal dramas. Genres can also be combined to form hybrid genres, such as the melding of horror and science fiction in the **Alien** films.

I am a genre lover - everything from
spaghetti western to samurai movie.

(Can you have a spaghetti samurai movie?)

To think about it more formally – we can say that genre films are those which share similar elements and can be identified by these elements. These elements can be referred to as paradigms meaning patterns of organisation, and we can show that audiences have certain expectations about what they will see.  Some viewers really don't like it if you mess with the paradigm.

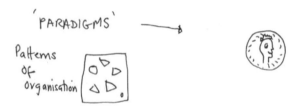

As Neale (1980) suggests, "Genre is a set of expectations". This is quite a clear way of putting it. Certain people love certain genres and watch them over and over again, for example TV genres of crime and murder, which seem to occupy most channels most of the time.

Some theorists argue that genres are actually cultural categories that are wider than the boundaries of film and media texts and operate within the organisation of industry, audience, and cultural practices as well. This means that we are talking about how culture is organized at the wider level within societies – which is a broader sociological approach.

As much as I love the Western genre, I
figured if I kept doing those, I'd
eventually run out of steam on that,
and that would've been the end of it.

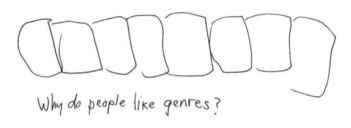

Why do people like genres?

Why do people like genres? Because it is deeply reassuring. This is
why children like some stories and repeat them over and over again -
it produces a psychological effect of recognition and safety.

Dad and kid:

> DAD
> What would you like to watch?

> KID
> **The Little Mermaid**, Daddy.

> DAD
> But you've watched it twenty times
> today already.

> KID
> But the Daddy in it is
> just like you, Daddy!

> CYNIC
> A 'genre' film is a film that follows
> a formula proven to bring in money.

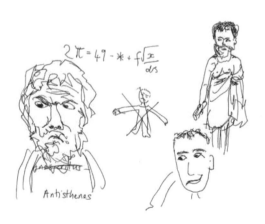

Manipulation

Audiences get emotional pleasures from genre films through recognition of narrative patterns. Genres evoke strong emotional responses through a kind of manipulation, using stylistic construction to evoke emotional responses, like horror, romance or comedy. In this way genre films are a kind of emotional release for the audience – which is what they pay for.

Audiences get...

Some genres, like the thriller, the 'whodunit' and the 'caper', offer the audience the pleasure of trying to unravel a mystery or a puzzle. The 'whodunit' is probably the oldest genre that there is. (Think of the Garden of Eden.)

emotional release

'Whodunit'

unravel a mystery or a puzzle,

Here is a rough list of the main genres – and the point is that, perhaps increasingly, genres overlap and permeate each other.

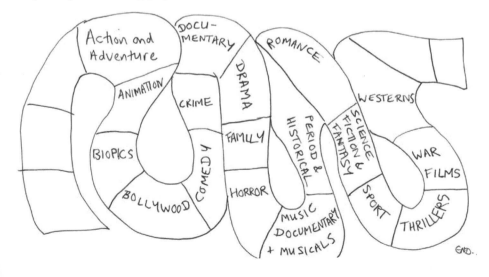

Action and Adventure — DOCU-MENTARY — ROMANCE — ANIMATION — DRAMA — CRIME — WESTERNS — BIOPICS — FAMILY — PERIOD & HISTORICAL — SCIENCE FICTION & FANTASY — WAR FILMS — COMEDY — BOLLYWOOD — HORROR — MUSIC DOCUMENTARY + MUSICALS — SPORT — THRILLERS — END.

- Action and adventure
- Animation
- Biopics
- Bollywood
- Comedy
- Crime
- Documentary
- Drama
- Family
- Horror

- Music documentary & musicals
- Period and historical
- Romance
- Science fiction and fantasy
- Sport
- Thrillers
- War films
- Westerns

(Ask yourself: how quickly can you spot a genre film once you start watching?)

## What the experts think:

GUNTHER KRESS

Genre is a kind of text that derives its form from the structure of a (frequently repeated) social occasion, with its characteristic participants and their purposes.

DENIS MCQUAIL

The genre may be considered as a practical device for helping any mass medium to produce consistently and **efficiently** and **to relate its production** to the expectations of its customers.

NICHOLAS ABERCROMBIE

Television producers set out to exploit genre conventions... It... makes sound economic sense. Sets, properties and costumes can be used over and over again. Teams of stars, writers, directors and technicians can be built up, giving economies of scale.

CHRISTINE GLEDHILL

Differences between genres meant
different audiences could be
identified and catered to... This
made it easier to standardise
and stabilise production.

KATIE WALES

Genre is... an intertextual concept.

JOHN FISKE

A representation of a car chase only
makes sense in relation to all the
others we have seen - after all, we
are unlikely to have experienced one
in reality, and if we did, we would,
according to this model, make sense
of it by turning it into another
text, which we would also understand
intertextually, in terms of what we
have seen so often on our screens.
There is then a cultural knowledge of
the concept 'car chase' that any one
text is a prospectus for, and that
it used by the viewer to decode it,
and by the producer to encode it.

DAVID BUCKINGHAM

Genre is not simply given by the
culture, rather, it is in a constant
process of negotiation and change.

ANDREW GOODWIN

Genres change and evolve.

CHRISTIAN METZ

Stages of genres: Experimental/
Classic/ Parody/ Deconstruction.

Lillin Gish

# Chapter 16 Stars and theories

Following on from mainstream ideas about genre, and the ways that audiences relate to the screen, or the story, we need to have a star-gazing interlude. That is to say we need to think a little bit about film stars and what they mean in film culture. From the very beginning there have been film stars: Lillian Gish, Mary Pickford, Charlie Chaplin and Rudolph Valentino. From almost the very beginnings of cinema the idea of stardom has been one of the industries defining characteristics.

```
               STUDENT
     What is a film star then?


               PROFESSOR
     Someone who is seen as a great actor,
     a star, an icon of the cinema.


               STUDENT
     They are like gods really, aren't they?
     They have this sort of magical aura.


               PROFESSOR
     Yep, it is charisma, a star-like
     quality that makes them more important
     than ordinary mortals. They are, as
     we say, larger than life. They are
     celebrities (i.e. people who are
     celebrated for being in movies).
```

HUMPHREY BOGART
If I wasn't a celebrity I'd
just be a 'has been'.


AUTHOR
Play it again, you ham.


Much film theory wanted to be serious about the importance and function of film, or to analyze its structure and elements. Intelligent theorists didn't want to think about film stars because they are so much a part of the studio industry and of Hollywood. They would say 'Frankly my dear I don't give a damn', but stars keep coming out whether you like them or not. They seem to be just part of the entire film business apparatus. Everybody loves a star. Creating glamorous stars is actually part of the publicity machine of Hollywood, and it clearly works, particularly today when we live in a celebrity-infested culture. It kicked off pretty early, probably between 1909 and 1912, and took off on the back of the way that celebrities had been created by the mass-market newspapers. Lindbergh the aviator was an early celebrity, as was Buffalo Bill, but once movies got going most stars were film stars.


JAYNE MANSFIELD
I am a movie star.

A film star, we might say, is a minor god-like figure that the public can identify with, and through whom they can live out their dreams. That is what being a fan means. Their appeal to our own identities is an important factor in the psychological attraction of stars. Richard Dwyer in the aptly named book *Heavenly Bodies: Film Stars and Society* has concisely analyzed this important phenomenon. Freud comes in here again in terms of the psychological relationship we develop towards figures of authority - or of charisma - which is what

154

film stars are. Basically the studio system created stars and owned and exploited them, from Mary Pickford right through to Marylin Monroe. The relationship which cinema has forged with its audience has been aided and abetted by the status of film stars, and the idea of celebrity. Stars remain the industry's primary marketing tool and are frequently an important reason for the audience's attendance in the first place.

```
            SUE MENGERS
        Stars are rare creatures, and not
        everyone can be one. But there isn't
        anyone on earth - not you, not me, not
        the girl next door - who wouldn't like
        to be a movie star holding up that
        gold statuette on Academy Award night.
```

'Star studies' is still in its infancy though, and is still partly dismissed by 'serious' film theorists.

```
            AUTHOR
        I doubt that film stars read
        film theory though.
```

# Back to earth...

The increasing arguments about the way in which film represents reality, people, sex and class, and in fact all aspects of social reality, led in the 1960s and 70s to more and more critical film theory. This kind of film theory was interested in questions like:

1. Is film part of an ideological apparatus?

2. In representing the real, does film partake of, and reflect, dominant ideologies?

3. Can film become part of a 'liberation' communication in which the nature of patriarchy, capitalism and repression is exposed?

4. How does film represent 'masculinity' and femininity'? – and are they constructs of ideology?

5. How is race represented in film? (Think back to *The Birth of a Nation.*)

6. How does film deal with issues of homosexuality, or any forms of non-conformist sexuality?

7. Is the dominant Hollywood narrative necessarily reactionary in its depiction of race and class?

8. Can radical films expose the nature of the dominant ideology through form, content, or critical editorial strategies?

As film theory began to develop a greater criticality, and a more thorough analysis of the relationship of film to society, it turned as a discipline to other philosophical approaches in order to develop new modes of thought. Philosophy and film had always had a complicated relationship, going back to Münsterberg, Eisinstein and Balázs, and now film theory engaged with new approaches, and in particular the theories of Realism, formalism, Structuralism, semiotics, Marxism, psychoanalysis, feminism, cognitivism, post-colonialism, Postmodernism, and gender and queer film theories. That is to say that after the 1970s film theory grew up, became an academic field of study and began to develop its own methods and means of analysis. The complexity of all of this film theory has produced huge amounts of work, some of it rather more difficult to understand than other parts, but the focus has always been to try and think through how films produce meaning, and how audiences understand those meanings.

Film theory grew up
AFTER THE
1970s

Unpacking all of these different approaches is a tricky business, and its not possible to cover everything, and anyway some people argue that you can sometimes have too much theory and that it can get in the way of looking at the films. That is, however, itself a theoretical position - but it is true to say that in the period of 'high theory' (the 1970s and 80s) film theory probably did become self-reflective and somewhat opaque and obscure. When film theory becomes too prescriptive it can seem that the theory thinks of itself as more important than the films - which is a concept too far!

Theory does not really make great movies and, as with music, the beauty of the performance cannot really be described in theory alone; you have to be there.

As Ingmar Bergman put it:


                    BERGMAN
        Film as dream, film as music. No art
        passes our conscience in the way film
        does, and goes directly to our
        feelings, deep down into the dark
        rooms of our souls.

* Cats eyes are small reflectors in
the middle of roads illuminated by
vehicle headlights

# Chapter 17 Semiotics and film

One key area of thought that impacted on film theory was Structuralism and semiotics - the science of signs.

Semiotics is about what signs and things mean. 'Everything is a sign and signs are everywhere' is the basic line.

What this means is that we don't just look at things, as things, like a rose, but we can see the rose as a sign. A rose is a rose, but it is also a sign for love and romance.

This basic observation that things can be a sign for something else is really a pretty radical idea, and it upsets quite a lot of people who like to think that the world is simple.

Interestingly, almost everything that is in a film is indeed there to be a sign (the mise-en-scène, the lighting, the gesture, the actor, the clothes, the background, the sounds, and so on).

```
There are the three wise
men following a star

Yep, that's a sign all right.
```

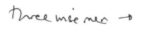

# Saussure and signs

Semiotics comes from the work of an obscure language theorist who taught in Geneva in the 1920s, although nobody paid any attention to him at the time, and he definitely didn't say anything about film theory!

What he did, in a quiet way, made a radical shift in how we think about the operations of language and meaning. Saussure said that if you think about it there are three components to the sign.

The sign- the signifier – the signified

The key point he made was that the relationship between the elements was not natural, not given by God, it was ARBITRARY.

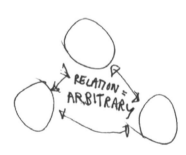

160

He said that you have the sign - the word donkey

DONKEY

you have the signified – donkey

and you have the concept - the idea of a donkey

(Why isn't a donkey called an Eeeh oor?) If you
see a donkey in a film and a guy with a palm leaf
what does that signify?

Next Saussure said that the important bit was that there are
different kinds of signs:

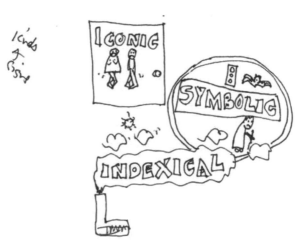

1. Iconic - a sign which closely resembles the signified (a portrait, a map, a diagram, a male/female toilet sign).

2. Symbolic - signs which do not resemble the signified but which are purely conventional (a stop sign, a red traffic light, or a national symbol like the American eagle).

3. Indexical - a sign which is connected in some way to the signified (e.g. smoke signifies fire, clouds signify rain, etc.).

Now the funny thing is that we discover that signs, like raising an eyebrow or even just smiling, can have all sorts of functions.

A sign can have a different function in different circumstances and that, my friends, is why it is all so applicable to films.

When we make films we put a load of signs together to try and signify something, and silent films in particular use a system of signification all the time – that is meaning is communicated through signs (and we all seem to know what they mean)

There is a famous 'sign' in Shakespeare's **Romeo and Juliet** when somebody says "Do you bite your thumbs at us, sir?" which is an insult, a sign of taking the mickey. If you suck your thumb, it signifies something quite different. And when you give a 'thumbs up' this also signifies something different again.

Semiotics (the science of signs) was drafted into film theory to allow for a more complex analysis of the way in which film images communicated with the spectators, and has been a fruitful means of thinking about film. Semiotic film theory was inter-woven with structuralist thought: so the ideas of Ferdinand de Saussure's semiology were integrated with Claude Lévi-Strauss's structural anthropology, to produce a complex structural analysis of how film worked. Then Umberto Eco and others tried to define film language as a set of codes and structures that organizes meaning in ways that are predetermined by the medium itself, rather than by individual filmmakers. This idea of the 'cinematic apparatus' was eventually codified by Christian Metz and became a highly influential film theory. (See later).

This was the high point of structuralist film theory, when everybody got into endless models, codes and patterns. For example in analyzing narrative cinema, Christian Metz came up with eight principal 'syntagmas', which were combinations of sounds and images organized into units of narrative autonomy - and from this you could analyze film scientifically (supposedly). In Britain people like Peter Wollen, Geoffrey Nowell-Smith, and others integrated Structuralism, genre studies, and auteurism into what came to be known as auteur-structuralism.

Like *The Bridge over the River Kwai* it might have been a structure too far.

# Feminist film theory

(How women
appear + don't
appear. ~)

Not talking about a man

# Chapter 18 Feminist film theory

Film theory, like a lot of other theory, had mostly been done by men (a basic point that feminists makes) and so at some point it became almost inevitable that a feminist film theory would arise. Most films were made by men, particularly mainstream and Hollywood movies, and women were portrayed basically, through the eyes of men. Feminism wanted to challenge the male world view, and in film theory to think about the way in which women were 'constructed' as female, by males.

Feminist film theory has emerged in the past 25 years to become a large and flourishing field, looking at every aspect of gender and film, and particularly how women appear, or often don't appear, in film. Early feminist film scholars, such as Molly Haskell and Sandy Flitterman-Lewis, focused on standard stereotypes of women in Hollywood and art cinema and sought to draw attention to previously neglected women filmmakers. Later scholars, like Mulvay, went further and sought to describe the patriarchal dynamics of cinematic spectatorship (how people watched movies).

Here is a great guide to seeing if films are male orientated:

The Bechdel Test for Films

1. There are at least two named female characters who
2. talk to each other
3. about something besides a man.

How many Classic Hollywood films would meet this criteria is a very interesting question.

STUDENT
But why do we need a
feminist film theory?

PROFESSOR
Well basically because we need an
explanation of why stereotypes about
men and women are endlessly reproduced
in films. Why men are always the
centre of films, why some films only
have men in them, why men dominate
the industry, why men get paid more
than women, and why the male point of
view of women as inferior, emotional
and sexy almost entirely dominates
mainstream cinema and TV. In film
women seem always to be passive,
pretty and preternaturally emotionally
intelligent, or dumb, or all of
that, and often looking for a man.

STUDENT
Is that all?

PROFESSOR
Well there is also the way that
reproducing gender stereotypes harms
children, and society, and reproduces
the dominant patriarchal ideology
in the interests of capitalism,
elites and, fundamentally, men.

STUDENT
Er, OK - that sounds like a
good argument. But what is
feminist film theory?

PROFESSOR
We could say that it particularly
looks at how women are presented,
described and defined in film.

W.C. Fields, the great drunk and misogynist, pretty much sets the
scene as to why we need a feminist film in this quote:

FIELDS
No doubt exists that all women are
crazy; it's only a question of degree.

166

A good counterpoint is:

JOHN LENNON
As usual, there is a great woman
behind every idiot.

# What is feminist film theory?

EVA GREEN
Most of the women in film are there to
be beautiful to the man.

Feminist film theory sets out to try and analyze and understand
why women are represented in a particular way in film, and why
this idea of women persists and is reproduced in film. It also tries to
develop theories of why men and women are thought of as being
fundamentally different, and why women are less represented in
film, and represented as being the lesser sex. These are complicated
issues and feminist film theory has drawn on many different
theoretical areas, going back to Freud, Marx and early feminism,
then bringing in Lacanian psychoanalysis, Althusserian Marxism and
semiotics.

The key points being theorized are:

- How subjects are created/formed through socialization and significatory processes (processes of representation).

- How gender is constructed/represented in film, through significatory processes.

- How men and women are 'positioned' by cinema. (The viewer as subject is placed/positioned in a particular way, as male or female.)

- Why film is so fascinating, and how it works so effectively to place men and women in preassigned gender roles.

# How feminist film theory developed

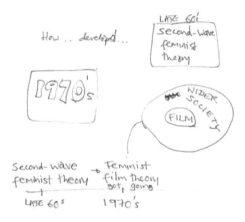

Feminist film theory really got going in the 1970s as a result of the development of second-wave feminist theory in the late 1960s, and began to look at film and the way in which it was a microcosm of the wider society. Women in mainstream film, as in real life, were presented as 'feminine' 'irrational' and the weaker sex, needing the protection of a man; you just have to think of John Wayne and his gloriously masculine patronizing of women in every film he ever made to get the point. In 1973 Claire Johnston edited a pamphlet called **Notes on Women's Cinema,** the first of its kind in the UK, and she was among the first feminist critics to offer a sustained critique of stereotypes using a semiotic point of view, that is to say looking at the idea of woman as a 'sign', and what femaleness 'signified' in cinema. This became a major preoccupation of feminist film theory.

I am not just a sex symbol.

Johnston put forward a clear argument about how classical cinema constructs the ideological image of woman. At its simplest, cinema was showing women as sexy and alluring, and at its more complex showing them as witty, sexy and alluring (or sometimes grumpy). Drawing on Roland Barthes's notion of myth, Johnston set out to investigate the myth of 'woman' in classical Hollywood cinema.

Key point - the sign 'woman' can be analyzed as a structure, a code or convention. (The way that 'woman' is shown becomes/ stands for an idea of what women are like in general - a sign for all womanhood.)

The sign can be said to represent the ideological meaning that 'woman' has for men. That is why Marilyn Monroe or Bridget Bardot become a 'star' or sign for all women.

In technical terms (drawing on semiotics, - the science of signs) we can say that, in relation to herself, the sign of woman means nothing as women are negatively represented as 'not-man'. (A man is a positive, active sign.) The 'woman-as-woman' is absent from the text of the film: she is an empty sign rather than a functioning character. Marilyn Monroe was, we might say, a pure signifier, a non-person, a 'woman'.

What is going on here in film theory terms is that, instead of thinking about cinema as reflecting reality, the idea is to think of cinema as producing a particular, ideological, view of reality. It is argued that classical Hollywood cinema hides its means of production and its ideological construction, through 'invisible editing' which produces an illusion. In this way, classical film narrative can present the artfully constructed images of 'woman' as natural, normal, realistic and sexy. This is the grand illusion of classical cinema. Thinking of woman as a sign replaces thinking of women as simply characters: the girlfriend, the lover, etc.

Laura Mulvey's now-classic essay *Visual Pleasure and Narrative Cinema (1975)* was probably the most important piece of work in this era. Mulvey (the godmother of feminist film theory?) was interested in the relationship between the screen and the viewer, in thinking about how the viewer was positioned. She stated the feminist claim that the 'male gaze' positions men and women differently in film.

# Key points of the argument:

1. Men are positioned as subjects who actively identify with the agents that drive the film's narrative forward: the heroes.

2. Women on the other hand are positioned as objects of beauty for masculine desire and fetishistic gazing. This is what the 'male gaze' means – the way that people look, and the desire that is in that looking. (Women, in this view, are passive.)

Or, to put it more simply it is about

1.   How men look at women

2.   How women look at themselves

3.   How women look at other women

Why...

STUDENT
Why are we so interested in the way
people look/the gaze in cinema?

PROFESSOR
Because we need to explain what
the fascination of viewing is,
and why watching films became, and
still is, incredibly popular.

Here is the opening sentence of the famous article:

MULVEY
This paper intends to use
psychoanalysis to discover where
and how the fascination of film is
reinforced by pre-existing patterns
of fascination already at work within
the individual subject and the social
formations that have moulded him.

Mulvey looks at how film positions the male viewer in particular.

Trying to understand the pleasure of viewing, Mulvey refers to the notion of (infantile) scopophilia, the desire to see, which Freud argued, is a fundamental drive. This drive is, like all drives, sexual in origin, and it is what keeps the spectator glued to the silver screen, enjoying the pleasures of Hollywood cinema. Viewing, watching and looking are basically enjoyable, and film manipulates this as much as possible. (Again, it is a fascinating question about how film has therefore affected culture.)

Self
regard
self-
love

According to Mulvey, Hollywood cinema stimulates the desire
to look by building structures of voyeurism (the desire to watch)
and narcissism (self-regard, self-love) into the story and into the
presentation of the image in film.

The argument is that voyeuristic visual pleasure is produced by
looking at another (character, figure or situation) as an object.

On the other hand, narcissistic visual pleasure can be derived from
self-identification with the main figure (the image) in the film -
again, think of action heroes/super heroes.

```
                    STUDENT
        This stuff is complicated. Why does
        it have to be so complicated?
```

PROFESSOR

Actually that is a good question.
The answer is that since the
**way film works, and people's**
reactions to it, are themselves
culturally complex, analyzing it
all is a complicated business.


STUDENT

What is being argued is that men and
**women view film differently, and are**
placed in different spaces by the
way that film works? Is that it?


PROFESSOR

I am tempted to say "Here's looking
at you kid", but that kind of gets
the main gist alright. We are talking
about 'spectatorship' by which we
mean how the viewer is positioned. In
the end the argument is that men and
**women are differently positioned. As**
Mulvey said, in a patriarchal society
"pleasure in looking has been split
between active/male and passive/
female" and it is understanding how
this works that is the basis of this
**strand of feminist film theory.**


STUDENT

But is it that clear about male and
**female? It sounds a bit black and**
white, if you know what I mean.


PROFESSOR

Well you have a point, and the article
has created a lot of controversy.
Basically, there was a big debate
**amongst film theorists about whether**
**the theory was too fixed, simplistic**
or technically essentialist, which
means that it talked about masculinity
**as if it was a fixed, single entity,**
and assumed that the female spectator
was similarly, simply, passive.

E. Ann Kaplan, another film theorist, put it rather acutely when she asked:

E ANN KAPLAN
Is the gaze male? That is, is the
operation of all film, at all times,
structured around a male gaze?

Kaplan and Kaja Silverman (1980), argued that in fact the gaze could be controlled or used by both male and female subjects in different ways.

- The male is not always the active controlling subject.

- The female is not always the passive object.

- The gaze can also be homosexual, not just hetrosexual.

- Spectators have some independence.

Teresa de Lauretis argued that we can in fact "read against the grain" - that the female spectator does not simply adopt the stated masculine reading position but is actually always involved in a complicated "double identification" with both the passive and active subject positions. Whichever way you look at it watching Bogart and Bacall on screen won't ever be the same again. And if you watch *Thelma and Louise* you might get a slightly different point of view.

# Julie Kristeva

One woman writer on film who has had quite an influence in recent times is Julie Kristeva, particularly for her ideas on the 'abject' and its relationship to horror movies. Again she is a complicated writer who comes out of a semiotic and psychoanalytic tradition and has written extensively on philosophical topics and theories of gender and language.

In relation to film she wrote a famous essay called **Powers of Horror**, in which she develops the idea and explains the importance of the abject. This idea is about the feelings of revulsion and horror that many people have at some time, and which don't seem to have any rational explanation. From the Expressionists onwards the idea of horror films has been attractive, and then morphed into vampire and other multiple sub-genres of horror. What is so interesting in the work of Kristeva is how she identifies this strange category of the abject, which had been little discussed, and shows how important it is to thinking about horror. She argues that the abject is constantly changing and is different for everyone, but that it is an important part of understanding ourselves as fully formed individuals within the symbolic order, the cultural sphere of the unconscious as it were. She defines he abject as "something so vile that I do not recognize it as a thing" - which is pretty strong stuff.

To understand the concept of the abject we have to think of the psychological moment when we separate ourselves from the mother, when we first recognize a boundary between our self and the other. We have to reject, to 'abject' the maternal, the living thing, which has created us, in order to be able to construct an identity. This later means that, on a repressed subconscious level, what was the maternal becomes and remains horrifying. It is from this ultimate abject moment, Kristeva argues, that we retain a fear of the abject throughout our lives. The irrationality of the abject haunts us like the terrifying fears of death, decay, vampires and other associated horrors.

Applying the abject in film theory is a productive sort of theorizing. In a now famous analysis, Barbara Creed applies Kristeva's theory of the abject to her discussion of the film **Alien**. She explains the way in which the film presents the female as both horrific and abject. So, for example, birth is shown as a horrifying process. The strange idea of a male being impregnated with a creature that then grows inside him, he who has no womb, and then rips itself free in a gloriously hideous shower of blood, is a remarkable feat of abjection. Creed argues that this is how film "abjectifies" female roles - a clear example of a film about how humans are forced to confront what they normally attempt to suppress.

This is a very interesting area of film theory which is much debated.

Kristeva's recent work on cinema widens the commentary still further. In a chapter of **Intimate Revolt: The Powers and Limits of Psychoanalysis**, titled **Fantasy and Cinema,** Kristeva discusses film as fantasy that "prompts us to take seriously this other reality - psychical reality." Talking about gender and film means discussing the role of fantasy, language and abjection within film theory, and takes us a long way from ideas of representing reality faithfully.

# Chapter 19 Third Cinema

THIRD CINEMA

# The politics of film

sometime...
in the late 1950s

The development of cinema in different countries and regions is fascinating, and the influences of early American and European film were felt in many ways. Some time in the late 1950s, a new kind of cinema began to appear in Latin America, one that drew on historical European influences but which had a strongly political outlook and which reflected the turbulent politics of the region. Cuba and the Cuban revolution, and the struggle for democracy and freedom in general, underpinned the ideas and intentions of this new kind of cinema. Basically the rise of cinema in developing countries went along with the struggle against colonialism of all sorts and with the rise of national cultures and identities. Overall, the 'Third Cinema' movement argued for a politicised filmmaking practice in Africa, Asia and Latin America, ever since its first appearance during the 60s and 70s, and has taken on board issues of race, class, religion, and national integrity.

ARGENTINA

Third Cinema began with various tentative initiatives in different countries, ranging from the emergence of Cinema Novo in Brazil, to the creation of a new Film Institute in Havana, Cuba, and the Documentary Film School of Santa Fe in Argentina. Cuban cinema is obviously related to the revolution and these revolutionary ideas, but the theory of filmmaking was also radical, seeking to break from traditional narrative and Hollywood.

```
                    CHE
      Lets make movies that kick ass!
```

# Towards a Third Cinema

***The Manifesto of the Third Cinem**a (1969)* was written by two Argentinian filmmakers Fernando Solanas and Octavio Getino and is one of those key texts in film theory that everyone should read.

They began with a quote from the anti-colonialist writer and theorist Frantz Fanon, who said:

```
                    FANON
      ... we must discuss, we must invent...
```

180

This is the opening paragraph that pretty much sums up what they are about:

SOLANAS & GETINO

Just a short time ago it would have seemed like a Quixotic adventure in the colonised, neocolonised, or even the imperialist nations themselves to make any attempt to create films of decolonisation that turned their back on or actively opposed the System. Until recently, film had been synonymous with spectacle or entertainment: in a word, it was one more consumer good. At best, films succeeded in bearing witness to the decay of bourgeois values and testifying to social injustice. As a rule, films only dealt with effect, never with cause; it was cinema of mystification or anti-historicism. It was surplus value cinema. Caught up in these conditions, films, the most valuable tool of communication of our times, were destined to satisfy only the ideological and economic interests of the owners of the film industry, the lords of the world film market, the great majority of whom were from the United States.

Third cinema

Anti-Hollywood, anti-fascist and pro-revolution

Latin America was heavily dominated by its powerful Imperialist neighbour , the USA, which consistently supported the right-wing military juntas. That is why third cinema was anti-Hollywood, anti-fascist and pro-revolution. Fernando Solanas and Octavio Getino argued in **The Manifesto** that this Cinema of Liberation "whose moving force is to be found in the Third World countries" was more than just a political movement - it was also an aesthetic movement that in some ways looked to Neorealism and other radical filmmaking ideas. In this argument however, First and Second Cinema do not correspond to the 'first' and 'second' world but represent a filmic geography of their own. For them First Cinema is the Hollywood model imposed by the American film industry, in other words the dominant industrial film model. And they argue that Second Cinema is that of auteur cinema, which in turn is not simply a European phenomenon, but is also found in places like Buenos Aires. In their view Second Cinema is only politically reformist and is incapable of achieving any lasting or profound change.

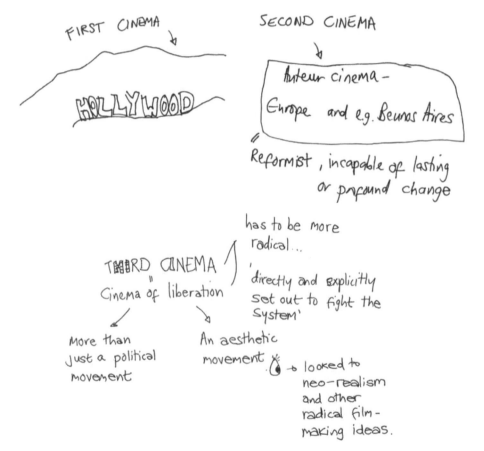

The only alternative to established cinema , in the face of the vicious repression of the fascist Latin American military dictatorships, they said, is a Third Cinema, consisting of films the system cannot assimilate, which "directly and explicitly set out to fight the system."

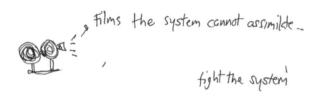

Films the system cannot assimilate...

fight the system

Third Cinema takes a different approach to filmmaking, by subverting cinematic codes, embracing revolutionary ideals, and combating the passive film-watching experience of commercial cinema.

# Key points on Third Cinema

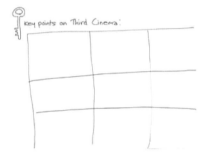

Key points on Third Cinema:

- Third Cinema has a clear political aim of liberation of the oppressed, whether based on class, gender, race, religion, or ethnicity.
- Third Cinema radically questions structures of power, particularly those of colonialism and neocolonialism.
- Third Cinema engages with questions of identity (who/what is a Cuban?), with national identities, and with the idea of community.
- Third Cinema deals with history, and challenges previously held ideas of the past, and seeks to uncover and show the 'hidden histories' of the oppressed.
- Third Cinema seeks to develop dialogue between the intellectuals and the masses by using film as a means of education and debate.

- Third Cinema challenges viewers to look at poverty by showing how it is lived, as in the neorealist approach.

- Third Cinema seeks to recover the idea of the nation - but a nation of inclusion - and to encourage the people to imagine new possibilities and directions.

- Third Cinema also reflects on diaspora populations who have been forced to leave their home countries through exile, persecution, or economic migration.

- Third cinema is always radical in both form and content.

Getino

Solanos

SOLANOS & GETINO
If we choose films as the centre of
our propositions and debate, it
is because that is our work front
and because the birth of a third
cinema means, at least for us,
the most important revolutionary
artistic event of our times.

If we are trying to sum up what Third Cinema was really like we can look at *La Hora de los Hornos (The Hour of the Furnaces)*, a film that runs for 4 hours and 20 minutes and is about the repressive political and economic situation in Argentina in the 1960s. This is "a militant cinema, involved ideologically and politically in and for the revolution."

La Hora de los Hornos'
1968

La **Hora de los Hornos** was the first film of its kind, made with and for underground militant groups - students, workers and guerrillas - in a country where the liberation of the revolutionary masses from a repressive military regime was in the making.

'We are not watching movies

SOLANOS & GETINO
We are not watching movies,
we are watching history being
changed through film"

After watching **La Hora de los Hornos** it is obvious that this film is not made for artistic purposes, but to become part of their revolution itself. It is revolution on the screen, and as such it is political action rather than entertainment. This is the radical idea of Third Cinema. The set-up of the movie begins with graphics and words flashing and beating onto the screen, inter-cut by clips of police brutality inflicted on demonstrators and civilians. The film is then broken down into different sections with titles and graphics, each about the revolution. The film is didactic, almost a lecture, but it is also an important medium of political communication.

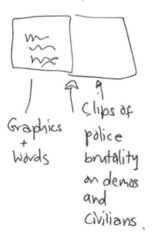

Graphics
+
Words

Clips of
police
brutality
on demos
and
Civilians.

For the first time, we demonstrated
that it was possible to produce
and distribute a film in a non-
liberated country with the specific
aim of contributing to the
political process of liberation.

The film therefore is not just an act of political courage; it's also a formal synthesis, a theoretical essay in filmmaking and a big influence on later film practice. The question of the political significance of film changes and develops but the underlying theoretical question of how to make effective radical film keeps coming back.

# Back to complicated European film theory.

# Chapter 20 Christian Metz

Christian Metz (1931- 1993)

A leading French film critic, he is one of those people who sought to produce a complete system, based in semiotics, for analyzing film. Following on from earlier work he then integrated psychoanalytical approaches into his system and established a complex philosophy of deconstructing film. This was during the 1970s when theory had

become a kind of high fashion, and everyone was trying to be more theoretically rigorous, and often more complex, than everyone else. Somebody said that the atmosphere at the time was 'heated' and this partly explains the rather bombastic tone that was adopted. Metz was instrumental in bringing film studies into academe, and for making film studies academically respectable; he certainly changed the nature of film theory. Where it all leaves us is another question however.

STUDENT
Did Metz make any good films?

PROFESSOR
Not that I'm aware of. He was
too busy writing theory.

STUDENT
Shouldn't the theory and the
practice go together?

PROFESSOR
I have no idea but then you can
definitely study things without
doing them - like the deep universe.

STUDENT
OK Prof, but what sort of
questions was Metz asking?

PROFESSOR
He had one very specific question
which was "What contribution can
Freudian psychoanalysis make to the
study of the cinematic signifier?"

STUDENT
That strikes me as a burning question
that everyone is dying to know the
answer to.

Metz's approach, it would be fair to say, is both complex and rigorous. He starts with the ideas of semiotics, where one looks at the signifying systems of a filmic production, then adds to this another level of psychoanalytical theory, based on Freud but also using the newly fashionable Lacanian re-reading of Freud. His complex theory is sometimes described as being centered on his 'apparatus' theory, which he developed in the 1970s. His works, in English translation, had a major impact on international film theory: *Language and Cinema (1971), Film Language: A Semiotics of Cinema (1974), and The Imaginary Signifier: Psychoanalysis and the Cinema (1977).*

This was the high point of Grand Theory, a term that was used to describe a period in which theory became admired for its own sake. We now probably inhabit a Post-Grand Theory era, where people entertain many different perspectives in film theory.

STUDENT
Was he anything to do with that
movie "Signifying in the Rain?"
That was really popular.

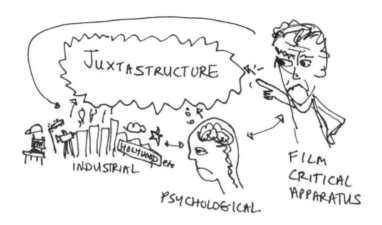

Metz's *The Imaginary Signifier* was his major contribution to incorporating psychoanalytic approaches in cinema studies, in an organized theoretical manner. Jean-Louis Baudry, for example, had previously written psychoanalytical film theory in regards to dream states and the cinematic apparatus, but Metz's *The Imaginary Signifier* took this approach to a new level of sophistication.

As we said, his name is now synonymous with the rise of modern, truly academic film theory, and is an interesting example of the way in which an academic discipline comes into being. He was a fairly hard-line structuralist and he led the movement that sought to create a pseudo-scientific structuralist apparatus that could say everything there was to say about film. In the current climate where scholars are starting to re-historicize film studies and film theory, it is necessary to see Metz's work in its historical context. Whether the theory is as useful as the structuralists claimed is now being openly debated. In a postmodern era where pretty much anything goes, it now seems almost quaint to claim to have devised a total system that explained everything about film.

# Metz is the Dennis Hopper of Structuralism

In essence, what Metz is trying to do is to create a cine-semiotics that can analyze the way that ideas are communicated in film, but in a way that scientifically understands the effects that the film has on the spectator, and he claims that the 'apparatus' of film operates in particular ways that can be described by a combination of semiotics and Freudian analysis.

This is a very ambitious theory to say the least, and the jury is out on whether all of the effort required to understand it produces results that are equal to the effort. To try and put it simply we can say that Christian Metz draws on the work of previous spectatorship theorists such as Jean-Louis Baudry and expands his own notion of the cinematic apparatus to encompass a more general view of 'the imaginary signifier' and its filmic institutional context. (Spectator studies attempts to understand the way in which the viewer reacts to, or is positioned by, film.) Metz's stated intention, through using psychoanalysis, is to "discover an original grounding event that would systematically explain the nature of the film spectator". This means to find a scientific explanation of the processes by which the spectator is inserted in the codes of the cinematic apparatus. The ultimate claim is that the mechanisms of the filmic apparatus mirrors that of the mind. You have to remember that at his point in film theory history the idea of the individual, the viewer, was seen as an ideological notion, a non-existent category which was actually only the product of 'structures'.

STUDENT
So, is Metz saying that the viewer
doesn't really make up their own mind?

PROFESSOR
That's pretty much it. The individual
is a kind of organized point of
resistance in the filmic apparatus
which controls it through structures
of ideology, psyche and filmic meaning.

STUDENT
It sounds a bit sci-fi to me, if
I'm enabled to make statements!

Ironically, it was Metz who said:

METZ
Film is difficult to explain because
it is easy to understand.

AUTHOR
Which just proves that you
can't trust film theorists.

191

To try and bring out the key points in Metz's argument we can say that by applying Freudian psychoanalysis to the actual film going experience, Metz focuses on a how a film satisfies three important desires: the desire for ego, the desire to desire, and the desire for the object through fetishism (ideas that derive from Lacanian psychoanalysis).

These three desires are only part, however of what Metz discusses within **The Imaginary Signifier** chapter. His apparatus is a complex theoretical model in which similar structures are found in the film, the mind and the audience.

# Ok, we'll try and summarize all of this

An important part of the institution of cinema is dependent on the actual technology of the industry (the equipment, modes of screening, the layout of film theatres, how audiences are organized, popular taste).

This is a product of society (in Marxist terms, the infrastructure and the ideological apparatus), but alongside it (juxtaposed to it) are certain psycho-physical determinations (how film acts on people).

It is the connection - what Metz calls the juxtastructure (sic) - between these two or three kinds of determinations that is of interest to Metz in studying the institution of cinema, which he then defines as the meeting of these three "machines": the industrial, the psychological and the film critical apparatus.

First of all there is the "external" industrial machine (the industrial and business practices of filmmaking, actual film distribution and exhibition, and the technology and the studio - Hollywood, etc.).

Then there is the "internal machine" of the controlled psychology of the spectator. (This machine interiorizes the dominant aspects of the industry – which Metz calls the political economy of cinema.) This happens through a "libidinal economy" in which there is an inter-related circuit of exchanges between the film and the spectator.

Finally, and rather bizarrely, he argues that film criticism is a third machine which is juxtaposed with the other two machines. He draws an analogy between the three systems and the three kinds of desire. This elaborate system has to be looked at further to be followed.

For Mr. Metz, Marxism, the (semio)-psychoanalytic, the political economy and the libidinal economy are all somehow on the side of science and knowledge, because they elucidate the ways that the cinema system operates in and through its audiences. It is their 'juxtastructural' relations which are the nub of Metz's complicated system - and it is up to the reader whether they go with it.

## Final note summary:

- Metz says that the cinematic signifier is imaginary because:
- It is fictional, that is, the image is created in support of narrative fictions.
- The cinema basically trades on the organized desire of the spectator.
- In a systematic way the symbolic and technological forms of cinema produce unconscious identifications in the spectator (fixing them in position).

## Juxtastructural may be the weirdest word invented in film theory

# Chapter 21 Representation, politics and identity

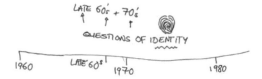

The politics of Third Cinema, and challenges to the dominant ideology, also arise in the area of film studies that deals with the idea of representation. This area of film theory is about how, and why, people are represented by particular identities in particular films. These kinds of question emerged from the political questioning and critical film theory of the late 1960s and 70s and were about what identity meant, and who got to define it.

Everybody has an identity, even if they stole it.

If we start at the beginning of film, we could ask about how Westerns constructed identities of the 'goodies' and the baddies' – and we all know who they were.

Cowboys were good guys, brave, tough, safe and noble whilst Indians were sneaky, dangerous, vicious and evil. This is what we mean by stereotypes - and the beginnings of the politics of representation. For a long time nobody thought about this process of representing people in particular ways in film and, as we have seen this was particularly true of women and of black people, and particularly in American films. From D.W.Griffith's appalling *The Birth of a Nation* right through to the classic *Gone with the Wind* the representation of black people in film was completely ideological, and completely racist. This is why 'representation' matters.

SPIKE LEE
People of color have a constant frustration of not being represented, or being misrepresented, and these images go around the world.

In the most general sense media representations are the ways in which film and media portray particular ethnic groups, identities, communities, experiences or ideas, from a particular ideological or dominant perspective. The question that has increasingly arisen in film theory is that of examining how these media representations serve to 're-present' or indeed to actually create a new reality. When film theorists talk about 'Realism' they often, as many of the French film critics claimed, mean talking about the dominant ideological representation of reality. When a film naturally represents men as more important, stronger, more decisive etc., it is in fact creating a kind of reality, not recording it. Lesbian and gay groups also began to seriously question the portrayal of sexuality in film, which was overwhelmingly and totally heterosexual. It was a world of black and white identities that failed to acknowledge difference in any meaningful way.

There is an argument that because film usually relies on simple narratives it has a tendency to deal in stereotypes, particularly in Classic Hollywood movies. The shorthand of film lends itself to certain kinds of representation and, more importantly, misrepresentation. Attention to these questions emerged from the 'politics of representation' - or identity politics of the 1980s. The ridiculous picture of the 'all American family' that had been the rule in Hollywood movies was subjected to much criticism, and new kinds of filmmakers began to develop an alternative cinema. Another important issue is that of 'whiteness', which is generally presented as the standard against which everything else is judged. Some theorists have argued that whiteness is 'invisible', that it is hidden by simply seeming to be the norm, which is what makes it so ideological.

Thinking about the nature of representation in film is like Pandora's box: once open, you can never close it again.

The world is a complex place, and the
influence of the media in its
representation and its power of
communication and interpretation is a
remarkable amplifier of emotions, and
of illusions.

TARIQ RAMADAN

As we said earlier when discussing feminist film theory, it is pretty obvious that the representation of women in films leaves something to be desired (actually 'something to be desired' is a pretty good description of the way women are represented, or misrepresented in film).

Gender is, of course, one of the most basic ways that people think about the world and it is a basic category of the way that reality is presented: there is male and there is female. An important question in the study of representation is exactly concerned with the way in which representations are made to seem 'natural'. This is how ideology works in film: things are presented as 'natural' and this powerfully reinforces the sense that the world is fixed and unchangeable. So the representation of people in particular ways can, and does, have political implications. This is what Spike Lee means when he talks about how people of color are shown in movies. For example, in many contemporary films it is pretty obvious that young, black men are portrayed as dangerous, violent and probably criminal. If you look at the history of film there is much evidence of the way different groups have been misrepresented, from the Jews in the 1930s, the Chinese in the same period, to the Irish and the Italians in the post-war period. Many of these kinds of representations are no longer acceptable, for obvious reasons, but the representation of women is still mired in the view of women as 'sex-objects'.

SPIKE LEE
Any film I do is not going to change
the way black women have been
portrayed, or black people have been
portrayed, in cinema since the days of
D.W. Griffith.

Thinking about the way that film produces representations can either be done at a simple quantitative level, as in how many black people are seen in movies in positions of power, or the numbers of women in movies altogether, or it can be analyzed in semiotic/signifying terms of what the representations mean. Both approaches are quite important in film theory. Think about how old people, teenagers, or any other category that you can imagine, are represented in film. The question is whether there are standardized, ideological, or partial representations of people or things in film, and what effect they have. To understand this we have to refer to the ways that film operates and the way that it conveys meanings, on many different levels, both manifest and latent.

STUDENT
OK, so how is masculinity
represented in movies?

PROFESSOR
From John Wayne to Sylvester Stallone
there is a basic image that goes: I
am male, so I am tough, I don't talk
much but I do a lot of stuff and in
the end I always sort things out.

STUDENT

Yessir, even I get that one: it is a
bit one-dimensional really, isn't it.


PROFESSOR

Things have changed but how
masculinity it portrayed is still a
basic problem. Some people even talk
about masculinity being in crisis.


STUDENT

Everything is in crisis these
days. There seems to be paranoia
everywhere, and movies just
get more and more weird.


PROFESSOR

That's what they call the Zeitgeist
(the spirit of the age). In fact
paranoia is probably the dominant
ethos in popular culture, along with a
general sense of alienation. The rise
of zombie and vampire movies tells us
something about the nature of human
relations in contemporary society.


STUDENT

These endless vampire movies
are a pain in the neck.


# This is how it works

In the analysis of representation there are two main approaches:
**Semiotics** and **Content Analysis** (a quantitative approach, which
means looking at the numbers behind various kinds of
representation, for example black people and women in films). As
we have said previously, semiotics foregrounds the process of
representation - it brings out the mechanisms.

Reality is always represented, not reflected - what we see as 'real' experience is always 'mediated' by perceptual codes. Representation, through its mediated nature, always involves 'the construction of reality.' There is no such thing as unmediated reality in film.

As representations become familiar through constant use they come to feel 'natural' and unmediated (stereotypes).
Representation is always selective, foregrounding some things and hiding others. While Realists tend to look at the way that representations relate to 'objective' reality (in terms of 'truth', 'accuracy' and 'distortion'), critical analysis focuses on whose realities are being represented and whose are being suppressed. Both structuralist and poststructuralist theories argue that 'reality' and 'truth' are the products of particular systems of representation – everything is organized and historically constructed. All representations require active interpretation - we respond to them because of the way they are framed.

# Some important questions about representation in film:

- What exactly is being represented? Or whom?

- How does it work? Using what sort of codes? What genre?

- Who controls the representation? Whose interests does it serve? How would you analyze this?

- Importantly, how is the particular representation made to seem 'natural' or 'true'?

- What is emphasized and what is suppressed? (How many women scientists are ever seen?)

- What is the audience that this representation is targeted at?

- How does a particular audience read a particular film?

- Is there a 'preferred' reading of a particular film?

- How do you think about the way in which a specific viewer understands a particular representation?

- How could film produce different representations?

- Are any representations 'natural' insofar as reality can simply be shown in film?

- In the postmodern world is everything a representation?

# Chapter 22 Postmodern film theory

Postmodernism is basically fragmentation, the belief that things no longer have a story, or a plot, or more simply that we have all lost the plot. In terms of film theory we can say that it is the idea that film should almost always be self-referential, that is to say that it should play with the idea of being a film. We are being flippant here because one of the characteristics of Postmodernism is said to be irony, or jouissance, or parody, or something of the sort. Postmodernism is to film theory what the ice-challenge is to politics, i.e. cold water poured on the heads of those who claim to have written definitive texts about what film theory means.

Basically modernist film was about being serious, cool, critical and alienated whereas postmodern film is about being witty, complex and filmically self-referential. That is why **Pulp Fiction** is the quintessential postmodern film; in fact it was made so that no-one else has to worry about being postmodern, we all just are. (David Lynch is pretty postmodern as well.)

The idea of what Postmodernism is has caused many arguments, and when, and how it started, is also very debatable. It can be seen as:

- A theoretical description of present day social reality.

- A collection of philosophical approaches to 'after' modernity.

- A literary and aesthetic movement in art, film, music, architecture and culture generally.

- All of the above (paradoxically).

# Defining Pomo (as cool theorists call it)

Postmodernism is one of the two or thee most unstable terms in cultural studies and philosophy today, as it is both an idea and a practice. So Postmodernism is probably best understood not as a rigid theoretical concept or a coherent ideological stance but as a bundle of shared impulses and tendencies amounting to a kind of common spirit. More than anything else Postmodernism is an attitude, and that attitude is definitively ironic. It revels in comedy and exalts the spirit of parody and play (see *Pulp Fiction*). It treats the monuments of tradition in particular with irreverence and derides the traditional distinction between artifacts of high and low culture. Postmodernism is also understood by some as a technological condition brought on by new electronic and mass media technologies, which have produced an entirely new culture (virtuality). Postmodernism definitely rejects the boundaries between high and low forms of art, elides rigid genre distinctions, and emphasizes pastiche, parody, bricolage, irony, and playfulness.

Postmodern art (and thought) favours reflexivity and self-consciousness, fragmentation and discontinuity (especially in narrative structures), ambiguity, simultaneity, and an emphasis on the destructured, decentered, dehumanized subject. This means the viewer adrift in a virtual world where all cultures seem to merge.

LARRY MCCAFFREY
This is the postmodern desert
inhabited by people who are, in effect,
consuming themselves in the form of
images and abstractions through which
their desires, sense of identity,
and memories are replicated and then
sold back to them as products.

The theoretical origins of Postmodernism lie in a rejection of grand theoretical systems, like those of Christian Metz, semiotics, Marxism and psychoanalysis, which claimed to have the answers to everything. Postmodernism says that these grand theories are inadequate to consider the complex, and contradictory nature of contemporary reality.

As Lyotard (seen as the grandfather of Postmodernism) said:

LYOTARD
... Simplifying to the extreme, I
define postmodern as incredulity toward
metanarratives.

From Jean-François Lyotard, *The Postmodern Condition: A Report on Knowledge.*

Jacques Derrida's ideas about deconstruction, which also rejected big theories and overarching ideas, played an important role in this as well. He appeared in a movie about himself where he (playfully) outlined his ideas.

Many people got annoyed by Postmodernism, claiming that it was vague and un-political and didn't lead to any proper analysis, although the films were quite good. Postmodernists were described by the old-school linguist Chomsky as:

NOAM CHOMSKY
Amusing and perfectly
self-conscious charlatans.

BRAD HOLLAND
In Modernism, reality used to
validate media. In Postmodernism,
the media validate reality. If you
don't believe this, just think how
many times you've described some real
event as being 'just like a movie.'

The debate about Postmodernism rages on but films that 'play' with the idea of film, reality and filmic sensibility are common place,. These films tend to anarchically challenge the ideas of narrative and realism, incorporating almost all the old tricks from the expressionists, formalists and the montage lot. Films like *Scream, Shaun of the Dead, American Beauty, The Matrix, Zombieland,*

*Being John Malkovich, Kill Bill,* are all fairly typical kinds of postmodern movie. We can loosely say then the postmodernist film tends to borrow from all previous genres, from all kinds of cultural frameworks, and throws everything together in ways that highlight the fact that we live in a very strange new post-internet world. Some theorists define Postmodernism in terms of a timeframe, as anything created after the 'modernist' phase of film.

Others describe Postmodernism as possibly a specific kind of style, starting with artists like Andy Warhol who used popular culture in order to create something quite new. Warhol recognized that we were entering a new era in which fame, popular culture and the cannibalization of all previous art forms was going to transform culture. He saw the power of TV and celebrity and, in his endless reproduction of images, was commenting on these phenomena. So Postmodernism as a style is often described as a renewed love of popular culture that remixes everything into new, entertaining pastiche. At the same time there are influences from gay culture in which camp and irony often arrive hand-in-hand with the postmodern style. Seriousness, in the modernist vein, is out the door.

Another good example is **Run Lola Run** which is an archetypal postmodern film in the way that it integrates animated sequences and also campy melodrama but still ends up being emotionally involving and entertaining. It is a kind of essay in film theory.

# Quick summary

Pomo is:

- A historical transformation of visual and narrative forms brought about by digital media.
- A filmic way of challenging the logic of binary oppositions (male/female, black/white, politics/culture, Western/Asian.)
- A new emphasis on the activity of the spectator that acknowledges the cultural and social specificity of spectators/viewers (does not see them as the 'mass').
- An interest in hybrid (inter-cultural) cinema and identity politics.
- A renewed interest in popular culture and its concerns.

- Cultural and aesthetic strategies of appropriation and pastiche that erode the distinction between the avant-garde and popular art. (*Pulp Fiction*)

- A disintegration of the distinctiveness of media (film, television, video, the digital arts). A creation of a complete postmodern virtual world of the spectacle.

Is *Blade Runner* a postmodern film, or is it sci-fi?

```
                    ZOMBIE
        How can vampires be postmodern
        when we are just dead?
```

# Chapter 23 Cognitive film theory

Cognitive film theory, like the cognitive sciences themselves, seeks to understand the exact processes by which people watch and understand films, from a practical and psychological point of view. This kind of film theory is very different from the political, structuralist and semiotic approaches that are concerned with the ideological effects of viewing. Cognitive film studies is concerned with the psychology of spectatorship and with the modes of audience comprehension and aesthetic understanding, in as scientific a way as possible.

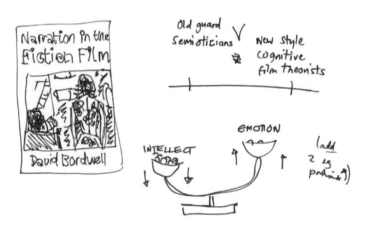

David Bordwell is considered to have brought cognitive theories into film in his work *Narration in the Fiction Film (1982)*. The approach is now well established. It is fair to say that there is a bit of a war between the new-style cognitive film theorists and the old-guard semioticians and the psychoanalytical film apparatus brigade.

# The main question is simply 'How do individuals make sense of feature films?'

Cognitive theory assumes that perception and cognition are universal human characteristics, so it does not take cultural or historical differences into account. This approach puts weight on intellectual rather than emotional aspects of watching film.

Interestingly some of the ideas go right back to Münsterberg – for example when he said we are looking for:

> MÜNSTERBERG
> ... first, an insight into the means by which the moving pictures impress us and appeal to us. Not the physical means and technical devices are in question, but the mental means. What psychological factors are involved when we watch the happenings on the screen?

Modern cognitive science is the name of a relatively new approach to understanding an old problem: the nature of the mind and mental activities, which had been an area much neglected in film theory. The study of film spectatorship - or at least the most interesting aspects of it - is looking at a conscious activity, rather than an unconscious 'positioning', as many had claimed.

The cognitivists argue that spectators can respond psychologically as if they were actually witnessing the events being projected before them in the film. However, they can do so in a way that demonstrates that they are aware of the nature of film.

> MÜNSTERBERG (CONT'D)
> They can respond with equal ease to the medium of representation as a medium of representation and to the world outside the representation as it relates to that representation.

In other words people know it is a film and respond accordingly, without necessarily being trapped in the illusion of film.

A very recent group called **The Society for Cognitive Studies of the Moving Image (SCSMI)** describes itself as:

```
                SCSMI
An interdisciplinary organization
made up of scholars interested in
cognitive, philosophical, aesthetic,
neurophysiological, and evolutionary-
psychological approaches to the
analysis of film and other moving-
image media. The society is on the
forefront of studying how moving-
image media shape and are shaped
by human psychological activity.
```

You can't say fairer than that.

Here is a neat quote from David Bordwell that pretty clearly sums up his position in relation to the more abstract, structuralist and meta-theoretical approaches to film theory.

```
              BORDWELL
Scholars often resist the cognitive
approach to art because they're
reluctant to mount causal or
functional explanations. Instead of
asking how films work or how spectators
understand films, many scholars prefer
to offer interpretive commentary on
films. Even what's called film theory
is largely a mixture of received
doctrines, highly selective evidence,
and more or less free association.
Which is to say that many humanists
treat doing film theory as a sort
of abstract version of doing...
```

... film criticism. They don't embrace
the practices of rational inquiry,
which includes assessing a wide body of
evidence, seeking out counterexamples,
and showing how a line of argument
is more adequate than its rivals.

In other words, he is arguing that film watching, and understanding, can be scrutinized like any other human activity, in a scientific and empirical manner.

# What do people actually do when they watch films and react to them?

# Chapter 24 Present day issues

STUDENT
Well, after all those different
theories the obvious question
is: where are we at?

PROFESSOR
Well, being flippant you might say we
are in the post-postmodernist moment.

STUDENT
I wouldn't say that. I'd say we're
in the cyber-digital age.

PROFESSOR
What does that mean?

STUDENT
You're supposed to know
everything. You tell me.

PROFESSOR
Well I guess we are saying that
film, TV, the web, everything is
coming together into a digital
universe where the differences between
film and TV are melting away.

STUDENT
Come, come, you must know by now that
you can't make sweeping statements
like that without backing them up,
making a clear analysis and stating
what sort of theoretical framework
you are using. It won't do.

PROFESSOR
I beg your pardon I just
thought I'd make a sweeping
generalization before lunch.

STUDENT

This is not a postmodernist film
theory book where flippancy rules OK!
We need a clear statement
of the position.

PROFESSOR

OK. Let me see, I think we can say
that film theory has undergone three
revolutions in the last twenty-
five years. First there was the
semiotic/structuralist revolution
where everybody tried to precisely
pin down how film worked on people,
the grand theory moment.

STUDENT

Which nobody really agrees
with anymore, right.

PROFESSOR

Well, the capacity of semiotics to
analyze the way things 'mean' in
film is still there, and important.

STUDENT

OK, but what else?

PROFESSOR

I would say that the second revolution
was the feminist and post-feminist
revolution which undermined the
big 'systems' of the Metz era
and re-opened the questions of
representation, control and political
diversity, in film and film theory.

STUDENT

So basically people began to see film
in a much less 'scientific' way and to
think more about global, political
contexts and influences, and what film
was doing amongst particular audiences.

PROFESSOR

I think that is right. So film theory
itself became more postmodern as it
were, which is probably a good thing.

214

STUDENT
And the third revolution?

PROFESSOR
Well I would say that it was an
historicizing revolution, where people
began to think about how film, and
film theory, developed and to look at
the ways this has influenced possible
modes of thinking about film. This also
comes back to looking at audiences and
how they relate to film, and funnily
enough today to how the audience can
actually almost be part of filmmaking,
through crowd-funding etc. The
world of film really has become more
democratic and open in some ways.

STUDENT
Yes, but Hollywood is still
there, is it not? And the
dream machine rolls on...

PROFESSOR
But even Hollywood now makes critical
films some days, and even lets women
make films, so something is changing.

STUDENT
And some people say that Hollywood
and Bollywood are converging,
that somehow world cinema is
becoming more inter-related, which
is also a good thing, right?

PROFESSOR
Indeed. World cinema is a growing
part of the film world, and people
are increasingly interested in other
countries - for example Iran, Nigeria,
Taiwan, India and China - and their
different kinds of filmmaking. So film
genres are becoming inter-woven in a
very postmodern way in the new global
world, the digital media worlds.

STUDENT

But where is film theory at then? Is
there an accepted view, or has it
all become hopelessly fragmented?
Is film now just part of the global
entertainment nexus that controls
popular culture, and it has all
become a 'selfie' culture?

PROFESSOR

Well, as we said film theory has
sort of fragmented: there is the
new cognitive theory line, there
are audience studies, post-colonial
film studies, hybrid film studies,
post-realist semiotic analysis
and history of film theory studies.
Basically film is so big that film
theory has about seven dimensions.

STUDENT

OK - but how important would
you say that film is overall?

PROFESSOR

The reality is that the digital/virtual
world has become so powerful there
is an argument, from Postmodernism,
and people like Baudrillard, that we
live in a 'simulacrum' of reality.
Film plays a powerful part in this.
(Think about how often people say "it
was like a film", which is what many
people said after the 9/11 bombings.)

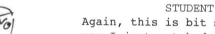

STUDENT

Again, this is bit sci-fi isn't it? Mind
you I just watched *Her,* and I sort of
know people like that. So maybe it is
happening, and we all think we live in
a film, a bit like a giant Truman show.

PROFESSOR

You are only as real as the people
you feel (or who you imagine exist).

216

OSBORNE
Ultimately a film theory is any kind
of theory that explains in some
way or other how films function as
films, as cultural messages, and as
cultural artifacts. So to be able
to read a film properly you need
to start thinking filmically.


THE END (FIN)

# Bibliography

Bazin, André. *What is cinema?* Vol 1 & 2. University of California Press, (3rd ed.) 2004

Bordwell, David & Thompson, Kristin (eds) *Film art: an introduction.* McGraw-Hill, 2010

Bordwell, David. *On the history of film style.* Harvard University Press, 1998

Colman, Felicity. *Film, theory and philosophy: the key thinkers.* 2010

Cook, Pam. *The cinema book.* (3rd Edition) BFI Publishing, 2008

Donald, James & Renov, Michael. *The SAGE handbook of film studies.* Sage, 2008

Dyer, R. *Heavenly bodies: stars and society.* BFI Publishing, 1998

Dyer, R. (ed) *Film: a montage of theories edited.* E.P. Dutton, 1966

Hayward, Susan. *Cinema studies : the key concepts.* 3rd Edition, 2006

Hoberman, J. *Vulgar modernism.* Temple University Press, 1991

Kael, P. *Reeling: film writings 1972-75.* Marion Boyars, 1997

Kracauer, S. *Theory of film.* Princeton University Press, 1997

Mackendrick, A. *On film-making.* Faber & Faber, 2004

McClintick, D. *Indecent exposure.* William Morrow, 1982

Monaco, J. *How to read a film* (4th ed) Oxford University Press, 2009

Nelmes, Jill. *An introduction to film studies.* 5th Edition. Routledge, 2012

Mamet, D. *On directing film.* Viking, 1991

Metz, C. *The imaginary signifier: psychoanalysis and the cinema.*
1986

Mitry, J. *Semiotics and the analysis of film.* 2000

Reisz, K. & Millar, G. *The technique of film editing.* Focal Press 2nd
ed, 2009

Roud, Richard. *Cinema: a critical dictionary.* Martin Secker &
Warburg, 1980

Sadoul, G. *Dictionary of films.* University of California Press, 1972

Sarris, Andrew. *The American Cinema: directors and directions 1929-
1968.* De Capo Press, 1966

Schatz, T. *The genius of the system: Hollywood filmmaking in the
studio era.* Faber & Faber, 1998

Schatz, T. *Hollywood genres: formulas, filmmaking, and the studio
system.* Macgraw Hill, 1981

Thomson, David. *A biographical dictionary of film.* (any edition)

Tarkovsky, A. *Sculpting in time: reflections on the cinema.* The
Bodley Head, 1986

Truffaut, F. *Hitchcock: a definitive study of Alfred Hitchcock.* Simon &
Schuster, 1986

Vogel, A. *Film as a subversive art.* Random House, 1974.

Walsh, M. *The Brechtian aspect of radical cinema.* edited by Keith
Griffiths, BFI, 1988

Wollen, P. *Signs and meaning in the cinema. New and enlarged
edition.* 1973

# Index

# A survivor's guide to student life
# By students, for students

Easy-to-use and essential, this up-to-date student's handbook has everything you need to know about making the most of your time at university. It contains practical, inside advice on all aspects of student life, and features a unique and indispensable academic primer for key areas of study. Sections include:

- Leaving home and getting organized

- Arriving, settling-in and making new friends

- Surviving Freshers Week

- Looking after your health and coping with stress

- How to study - coursework, exams and essays

- Key subject areas - what you need to know

- Thinking about the future – what next?

223